Wisdom Has Built Her House

Studies on the Figure of Sophia in the Bible

Silvia Schroer

Translated by Linda M. Maloney
and William McDonough

A Michael Glazier Book
THE LITURGICAL PRESS
Collegeville, Minnesota

A Michael Glazier Book published by The Liturgical Press

Cover design by Ann Blattner. Cover illustration: The Goddess Maat with an ostrich feather, symbol of air and light. Fragment of a relief from the tomb of Sethos I (ca. 1300 B.C.E.), in Florence. Photo courtesy of Othmar Keel.

Originally published as *Die Weisheit hat ihr Haus Gebaut,* Matthias-Grünewald Verlag, 1996.

Biblical citations, except where otherwise indicated by an asterisk (*), are from the *New Revised Standard Version Bible,* © 1989 by the Division of Christian Education of the National Council of the Churches of Christ in the United States of America.

1	2	3	4	5	6	7	8

Library of Congress Cataloging-in-Publication Data

Schroer, Silvia, 1958–
    [Weisheit hat ihr Haus Gebaut. English]
    Wisdom has built her house : studies on the figure of Sophia in the Bible / Silvia Schroer ; translated by Linda M. Maloney and William McDonough.
        p.   cm.
    Includes bibliographical references and index.
    ISBN 0-8146-5934-9 (alk. paper)
    1. Wisdom (Biblical personification). 2. Feminist theology. I. Title.

BS580.W58 S37 2000
223'.06'082—dc21

99-088429

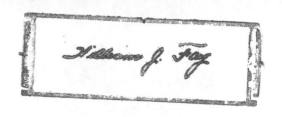

Wisdom Has Built Her House

For Othmar

Contents

Foreword

The nine essays on personified Wisdom (Hebrew *Ḥokmā,* Greek *Sophia,* Latin *Sapientia*) here collected for the first time were written over the course of ten years. The first appeared in 1986, while the two most recent were written for this book. Updatings are placed in each case at the beginning of the notes and marked with an asterisk (*). The sequence of chapters is not determined by their original dates of appearance, but by the originating dates of the biblical writings discussed. The theme of "Wisdom" has never let go of me through these years, even if it was not always central to my work. I, like many others, have my teacher Othmar Keel to thank for my interest in the figure of Wisdom. As early as 1974 he published a very intriguing little book on personified Wisdom in Proverbs 8:22-31, and it was he who was clever enough to detect the Ancient Near Eastern dove symbolism in the New Testament's accounts of Jesus' baptism at the Jordan as well. Further impulses were supplied me by the books of Claudia Camp and Max Küchler, and—on the subject of Christian reception of Wisdom theology—above all by Elisabeth Schüssler Fiorenza. Teaching opportunities in Fribourg and Bern gave me further opportunities to demonstrate the connection between the image of women and the Wisdom image of God in Israel, and to discuss this with my students. The findings that resulted from this long process came together in lectures and articles, for example in my professional qualifying lecture on the theme "Wise Women and Counselors" (1989) and in a lecture on "Wisdom and Postexilic Monotheism" for the working group of Catholic women Old Testament scholars in Luzerne (1990).

At the same time my principal professional occupation was directing adult biblical education programs for the Swiss Catholic

Biblical Association. It was never difficult to awaken interest in this theme of personified Wisdom in parishes, deaneries, working groups, and above all in women's groups. There were unforgettable workshops, weekends, worship services, and women's retreats on the theme of Wisdom. An issue of the journal *Bibel Heute*, which I edited with other women on the theme of "Sophia—God in the Image of a Woman," enjoyed such large sales in such a short time that it was reprinted and distributed as part of the documentation for the Women's World Day of Prayer. Conversations and Bible studies with many women and men in the Church and often with others marginal to the Church were a kind of touchstone for my scholarly exegesis on this theme. Above all they exerted a healthy pressure on me to reflect, always in new ways and concretely, about the context and goals of my biblical theology. That so many of the ideas first developed in the following essays have been taken up and transformed for pastoral uses is what pleases me most. I was also delighted by a very exciting debate on the plausibility of a Wisdom christology that Luise Schottroff and I enthusiastically conducted in January 1995 in Arnoldhain before a packed audience. The essay "The Spirit, Wisdom, and the Dove," which is not so easy for non-specialists to read, appeared first in a scholarly journal in Fribourg (Switzerland) and played an important role when the bishop of Rottenburg refused to grant me a teaching position for introductory Old and New Testament exegesis. I have never modified or corrected the theses and formulations defended in this essay, either in writing or orally, in order to re-open one of the portals to the empire of Catholic professorships. I am neither so presumptuous nor so naïve as to believe that my reconstructions of the tradition-history of a symbol are absolutely "objectively" right or irrefutable. Many things are of course open to discussion, but not when (pretended) theological discussions are misused as bare instruments of power. That many Catholic women theologians are ready to bring the required tribute and to give in to the demands of bishops or Roman authorities in order to obtain a teaching position I take to be a very regrettable development, one that discredits feminist theology at its core, especially if it has any interest at all in being regarded as a special form of liberation theology. Wisdom has thus had a remarkably powerful direct and indirect influence on my life. She fills me even now with many images, with power for resistance, with commitment to justice, with laughter, and with *eros*.

There were many reasons for my decision to collect into one book a set of essays that, because of the different ways in which they originated, are not completely homogenous. For one thing, some of these essays appeared in books and journals that are very technical or have since gone out of print and are thus inaccessible to a broad audience. For another, none of these essays has become so outdated in the course of further discussion that it has by now earned its rest in the archives. I thank Mr. Bruno Kern for the inspiration for this book and for his advice as I was putting it together. I want to dedicate this little volume to my teacher and reliable friend Othmar Keel, who has guided my writings and activities in Wisdom for sixteen years, who has been unobtrusively interested in my path, and who has been like a firm rock in the dashing waves of my life. Sophia knows how much I owe to him!

Köniz, on the feast of Divine Wisdom, Pentecost 1996
Silvia Schroer

CHAPTER ONE

Wisdom on the Path of Righteousness
(Proverbs 8:20)

The figure of personified Wisdom made its first appearance in postexilic Wisdom literature, but it would be a mistake to regard it as isolated within that period, for despite its late appearance this figure is firmly established within Israel's whole tradition of written wisdom, which is of course older and was recorded primarily in the central and principal section of the book of Proverbs (chs. 10–30). Moreover, it stands in very close relationship to the likewise older goddesses of Egypt and western Asia, whose images and cultural contexts have shaped the figure of personified Wisdom. We should emphasize her relationship with the Egyptian Maat and, in the Ptolemaic-Roman period, with the goddess Isis, who took on many aspects of Maat. For the most part these backgrounds and contexts cannot be fully presented in the essays collected here. Nevertheless they are of great significance as historical confirmation especially for a feminist-theological reconstruction of the history of Israel's faith, and I am convinced that they may even provide the most important key for a contemporary feminist reading of many Wisdom texts.

1. Faith in the Connection between Action and Consequence— Or the Ancient Near Eastern and Israelite Belief in Justice Before Death

In the Ancient Near East, as in Israel, there was a basic ideological model that today we like to call the "connection between action and consequence." In this view of the world the good or evil deeds of a human being created a kind of sphere of action that automatically brought about a good or bad life result for the individual or also for the group—for the individual's tribe or people. The idea of collective liability was not foreign to the Israelites (see Exod 20:5-6; Deut 5:9). The Deuteronomistic writers used it to explain the catastrophe of the exile as the consequence of the people's sins (Leviticus 16; Deuteronomy 28, and elsewhere). Ezekiel and Jeremiah vehemently attacked any connection between guilt and its consequences extending over generations, and pleaded for individual liability (Ezek 18:3-20; Jer 31:29-30). Wisdom appears always to have had the fate of the individual more sharply in view, as these examples from the book of Proverbs show:

> The righteousness of the blameless keeps their ways straight,
>   but the wicked fall by their own wickedness (11:5).

> Whoever is steadfast in righteousness will live
>   but whoever pursues evil will die (11:19).

> No harm happens to the righteous,
>   but the wicked are filled with trouble (12:21).

> The righteous have enough to satisfy their appetite,
>   but the belly of the wicked is empty (13:25).

This Wisdom conviction that the order of the world functions according to moral laws and that the keeping of those laws is supervised by divine powers was in a certain manner irrefutable and led to the (tragic) inference that behind every piece of bad luck and every illness was the conscious or unconscious guilt of the sufferer or his or her parents (cf. also Luke 13:4 or John 9). Experience, of course, confirmed this axiom only among groups of people who were free and more or less well-situated, and even there only to some extent. In every age there have been scoundrels for whom everything has gone splendidly right up to their deaths, and there have always been righteous people dogged by bad luck. In times of political, social, or religious crisis, when the old order no longer applied and chaos triumphed, this discrepancy was apparent even in those groups that in normal times could rely on the experience that with diligence, wisdom, loyalty to the community, and other highly-prized virtues one would not fall so suddenly into misery and decline. Out of this tension between belief and reality came the "Laments" written in Egypt at the end of the third millennium B.C.E. about the general decay of order. In Israel the book of Job documents this so-called "crisis of wisdom"—which was really a thoroughgoing crisis in the economy, politics, and religion—in the form of a very frank Wisdom treatise. However, many of the Psalms attest, from the perspective of the man or woman praying, the distress of someone who wanted to believe in the connection between action and result, that is, in justice before death, but who encountered great misery even though he or she was a righteous person (e.g., Psalms 10; 37; 53; 64, and many others). In fact, the connection between action and consequence remains a central theme in all the Wisdom writings, including the late book called "Wisdom," and all, with the exception of Qoheleth, in wrestling with this faith in a greater justice come finally to the conviction or recognition that there is a just order and that Israel's God YHWH is its highest guarantor.

Ḥokmā or *Sophia* as divine symbol represents this just order, among other things, and she pleads untiringly in the book of Proverbs for faith that the path of righteousness, communal loyalty, and truthfulness is the better way, even if the "godless" with their unscrupulous intrigues profit in the short run and live in prosperity. We find here a meditation extending over centuries on an inner-worldly justice that will be visibly realized in the lifetime of this generation or its children. The book of Wisdom (from the first century B.C.E.) is the first to introduce the idea that the fullness of justice will be postponed until a life after death.

2. The Ethical Order as Part of a Cosmic Order

Within the Israelite symbol system personified Wisdom corresponds almost exactly to the Egyptian goddess Maat. A few years ago, in his distinguished monograph, Jan Assmann[1] used the example of this central goddess figure and idea to illustrate the Egyptian worldview. Maat is the world order, pure and simple.

Accordingly she encompasses the divine and nature, the royal realm, society, and human relationships. She stands for the cosmic and the divinely-willed, and that means the ideal cultural order. Her image is found wherever that order is at stake: for example, on scales that should show the correct weight, or on musical instruments that produce harmonic tones (see Figure 1), or as a pendant around the neck of the judge who is to pronounce judgment. As a goddess Maat belongs to the Egyptian pantheon, but she has a special position because the other deities are oriented to her as the cosmic principle. Thus Maat is the tutelary goddess of Osiris, the god of death, and of the dead, since she represents the order that they must prove they have kept, when they appear before the judgment seat in the world to come (see Figure 2). As a tree goddess she offers shade, food, and drink to the dead in the next world (see Figure 3). Maat is considered the daughter of the sun god Re. She stands in the bow of the sun's boat, because Re accomplishes the cosmic order of the sun's course, an order ordained by Maat (see Figures 4 and 5). Maat is one of the patron deities of royal authority (see Figures 6 and 7), because the king is the guarantor of the divinely-willed cosmic and social order that makes human life possible in the first place. Thus in the cult the king brings Maat as an offering to the gods (see Figure 8), which means he stands in for Maat as her proxy and acts as guarantor for her, since the gods do not directly intervene in the unfolding of events. The opposite counterpart of Maat is Isfet, the condition of lawlessness, violence, and oppression. The social order Maat represents is not democratic, but hierarchical, yet the law she represents is the law that gives the weak a chance; it is the idea of a vertical solidarity of the better-off with all parts of society.

It has been shown that Israelite sages knew and received Egyptian Wisdom teaching. So, for example, in the book of Proverbs (22:17–23:11) a section from the Egyptian Wisdom teaching of Amen-em-ope has been taken over with only insignificant modifications. That these same sages sketched the figure of personified *Hokmā* with different accents from the model of Maat is obvious. Like Maat, *Hokmā* stands like a goddess next to the creator God and is co-creator of the cosmos. Of course, it was not only the image of Maat that influenced Prov 8:22-31. The more playful aspects may be traced to Hathor and the figure of the divine consort,[2] probably in large part also to the Syrian and Canaanite tradition of the erotic goddess who presents herself before the storm god of the enthroned sovereign.[3] Like Maat, *Ḥokmā* is linked in a special way to the kingship, for her appeals are directed principally to the powerful (Prov 8:15-16; see also Wis 6:1-11).

Job 28 presents *Ḥokmā,* as does the Egyptian tradition, as a kind of blueprint for the world, as cosmic order (similar to Wisdom 7 and 8). This chapter in particular shows, in the context of the whole book, that *Ḥokmā* or *Sophia* as a personification is actually a symbol of the theology of each individual writing. The book of Job and its protagonist wrestle most intently with the question whether a rational and just order really undergirds this world. That order threatens to slip away from Job (and thus from all true sages). Hence it is not surprising to find in Job 28 such urgent inquiry about the place where Wisdom dwells, and such powerful contention over whether she is accessible to human knowledge at all. God's speech in Job 38–41 finally responds to Job's questions and his accusation concerning the lack of a plan for the world with a detailed description of the order of creation.[4] In this order of creation not everything is centered on human beings. The wild animals, who are not useful to humans, also have a right to life. The existence of such realms of chaos conforms to the divine plan. At the same time it is made clear that God does personally control these dangers and that God's justice proves itself in constant battle against wrongdoers and evil. The theme of justice and suffering because of injustice is typically treated in Ancient Near Eastern thought as a cosmic concern. As a single human being Job stands within a universe to which the stars also belong.

The Wisdom of the First Testament, like Egyptian Maat, cannot be separated from the *idea* of an all-encompassing just order and the *doing* of justice. *Ḥokmā* is prophet and teacher of righteousness; the study of Wisdom serves *ṣedeqā;* indeed, Wisdom is the inner side of righteousness, as it were. Thus the introduction to the book of Proverbs begins with verses that establish precisely this mutual relationship among wisdom, justice, right, and equity (Prov 1:2-3). In the speech of *Ḥokmā* in Prov 8:1-21 the root *ṣdq* appears no less than five times (see vv. 8, 15, 16, 18, 20). The book of Wisdom also places the appeal for righteousness programmatically at the beginning (Wis 1:1). The Israelite idea of *ṣedeqā* places the accent on the social aspect of righteousness. The Egyptian notion of Maat is broader and implies the cosmic and natural orders as well. Certainly the biblical texts are also aware of the mutual dependence of the harmony of society and cosmos. When justice is corrupted a drought breaks over the land (Hos 4:2-3); when the envoy of YHWH reestablishes righteousness, the whole created order is newly fitted together: "The wolf shall live [as a guest] with the lamb, the leopard shall lie down with the kid" (Isa 11:1-9). The book of Job leads its protagonist out of the strait into which suffering had driven him into the broad spaces of God's creation. The book of Wisdom dreams that at some time in the future God will go forth to battle against the foolish and the ungodly with the help of all creation (Wis 5:14-23).

3. Through Wisdom to Righteousness: Starting Point for a Feminist Theology

It seems to me that this Egyptian and Israelite idea of a just order that embraces and takes its starting point from the cosmic and social sphere, and in which a disruption in one realm unfailingly leads to a break in the harmony of the other realm, offers an extraordinarily provocative impulse for a feminist theology that would begin with the necessity of a world-encompassing justice and from there develop a theology of relationship, an eco-feminist theology, and so on. The advantage of this recourse to the biblical traditions lies among other things in not merely associating justice with individuals, but always seeing it in a much larger context. In addition, in contrast to other biblical traditions Wisdom teaching does not declare the human being the center or crown of creation (see both Job 38–39 and Psalm 104), which is entirely contrary to the initiatives of a feminist anthropology and ecology. The teacher of social and cosmic, i.e., nature-inclusive justice is *Ḥokmā,* the wisdom of women, itself an image of God. One may want to object that Israelite *Ḥokmā,* like Egyptian Maat, was fused with the Wisdom images of the ruling classes, with a hierarchically organized class society revolving around a king. However, I do not find this objection completely justified. After all, these Wisdom texts addressed themselves directly to the powerful, to those with responsibility for society, and appealed to their consciences—evidently still present. They still presume that a land only had a future if the young were educated in wisdom and righteousness; even then, so long ago, they derived human rights and human dignity from the fact that all human beings were created by the same Creator (Prov 14:31; 17:5; 22:2). These writings presuppose that human beings are never relieved of the obligation to desire what is good for all. Maybe it is time for us to come down from our high horse, from whose lofty back we are used to looking down on ancient cultures as primitive, pre-enlightened, pre-democratic, and thus irrelevant as far as their ethical notions are concerned. The desolate condition of the world and of our Western civilization does not permit such arrogance. In any case, the gain we may derive from this ancient Near Eastern Wisdom thinking for very pressing questions today should be unexpectedly great. It is worthwhile to preserve these traditions, to test them, and to reshape them.

NOTES

1. Jan Assmann, *Maat. Gerechtigkeit und Unsterblichkeit im Alten Ägypten* (Munich: Beck, 1990).

2. Othmar Keel, *Die Weisheit spielt vor Gott. Ein ikonographischer Beitrag zur Deutung des m^esahäqät in Sprüche 8,30f* (Fribourg: Universitätsverlag; Göttingen: Vandenhoeck & Ruprecht, 1974).

3. Urs Winter, *Frau und Göttin.* OBO 53 (Fribourg: Universitätsverlag; Göttingen: Vandenhoeck & Ruprecht, 1983).

4. Cf. Othmar Keel, *Jahwes Entgegnung an Ijob. Eine Deutung von Ijob 38–41 vor dem Hintergrund der zeitgenössischen Bildkunst* (Göttingen: Vandenhoeck & Ruprecht, 1978).

Figure 1
The head of the goddess adorns a harp whose harmonies are part of the greater order of things that she herself governs.

Grave painting from western Thebes (ca. 144 B.C.E.), from: Othmar Keel, *Die Weisheit spielt vor Gott* (Fribourg: Universitätsverlag; Göttingen: Vandenhoeck & Ruprecht, 1974) Figure 22.

Figure 2

At the judgment of the dead the heart of the dead person will be weighed against Maat who crouches on the scale. Frequently Maat herself is also the mistress of the scales. On this papyrus the jackal-headed god of death Anubis has taken over this office. Behind him stands a double image of Maat. This doubled image reinforces the validity of her witness at the judgment, for it is she who tests the veracity of the negative confessions of sin by the dead.

From the Greenfield papyrus in the British Museum, London (1075–944 B.C.E.), from: Alexandre Piankoff and N. Rambova, *Mythological Papyri*. Bollingen Series 40:3. Egyptian Religious Texts and Representations 3 (New York: Pantheon, 1957) Figure 37.

Figure 3

Beginning with the twenty-first dynasty (1075–944 B.C.E.) the tree goddess—who since the eighteenth dynasty is depicted in papyri and grave paintings refreshing the dead with food and drink—is identified with the goddess Maat. Here she is identified by the ostrich feather; she appears as a figure of a woman drawn within the tree and giving gifts to the dead.

From a sarcophagus painting in Turin, from: Othmar Keel, *Das Recht der Bilder gesehen zu werden.* OBO 122 (Fribourg: Universitätsverlag; Göttingen: Vandenhoeck & Ruprecht, 1992) Figure 95; see also Figure 96.

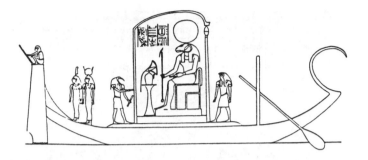

Figure 4

Maat and Hathor stand in the bow of the boat of the ram-headed sun god Amun-Re.

Relief from the Holy of Holies of the temple of Ramses II in Wadi Sebua (circa 1250 B.C.E.), from: Keel, *Die Weisheit spielt vor Gott*, Figure 25.

Figure 5

Together with Hathor,Maat (standing on the right, with the ostrich feather) guards the solar disk in her boat. At the same time she is seen standing inside the solar disk, worshiping before the throne of the sun god Amun-Re.

From the breastplate of King Sheshonk II of Tanis (10th c. B.C.E.), in Cairo, from: Urs Winter, *Frau und Göttin. OBO* 53 (Fribourg: Universitätsverlag; Göttingen: Vandenhoeck & Ruprecht, 1983) Figure 515.

Figure 6

Maat is the tutelary goddess of the king and the royal realm, and thus she is depicted in intimate association with him. Here she is depicted with Tutankhamen.

From the counterweight of a breastplate from the treasury of Tutankh-amen (1336–1325 B.C.E.), in Cairo, from: Urs Winter, *Frau und Göttin*, Figure 516.

Figure 7

The goddess supports the king—here Tutankhamen—in his service of the gods. The Pharaoh brings a sacrifice of flowers and drink to Re-Harachte. The goddess with the ostrich feather, who herself symbolizes this order, holds him under the arms.

From a depiction on one of the shrines from the tomb of Tutankhamen, Cairo, from: Alexandre Piankoff and N. Rambova, *The Shrines of Tut-Ankh-Amon* (New York: Pantheon, 1955) 117, Figure 39.

Figure 8

In worship, the king brings Maat in her typical squatting posture as an offering to the gods, here depicted as the falcon-headed sun god Re-Harachte.

Scene on one of the columns in the second hypostyle hall of the temple of Sethos I of Abydos (1290–1279 B.C.E.), from: Alan H. Gardiner, Amice M. Calverley, and Myrtle F. Broome, *The Temple of King Sethos I at Abydos* (London: The Egypt Exploration Society; Chicago: The University of Chicago Press, 1933–) vol. IV (1958) Plate 7.1.

CHAPTER TWO

Divine Wisdom and Postexilic Monotheism*

Since its beginnings feminist theology has been interested in the figure of the goddess in Israel and in the few images of YHWH as a mother in the Bible. However, it has concerned itself only recently (and then peripherally) with what is certainly the most developed female image of God in the biblical writings, namely personified *Hokmā*. In 1986 an initial monograph appeared in North America with the title *Sophia: The Future of Feminist Spirituality*.[1] Otherwise *Sophia* ekes out a bare existence, appearing mainly under inappropriate chapter titles like "God, our Mother,"[2] or "The Appropriation of the Goddess in Jewish and Christian Monotheism."[3] While numerous studies have given minute attention to the meaning of *ruah*,[4] feminist remarks on Wisdom often mirror the same bewilderment about this figure that is to be found in traditional exegesis. Women's interest in *Sophia* focuses on her femaleness or her similarity to the goddesses, but one author regards her as a "[relic] of a cult of female deities in the ancient Near East,"[5] while another refers to "divine *Sophia*" as "Israel's God in the language and *Gestalt* of the goddess,"[6] and still others, although perceiving the goddess behind "this powerful image of Wisdom" assert that "in Hebrew thought she has become a dependent attribute or expression of the transcendent male God rather than an autonomous, female manifestation of the divine."[7] It is noteworthy that up to the present time there have been very few European feminist exegetical contributions on the subject of personified Wisdom that investigate this figure in the context of the individual writings—that is, using the methods of historical-critical analysis.[8] North American publications reveal a different profile;

their scholarly quality is attested, for example in the field of Second Testament studies, by the presence of authors such as Elisabeth Schüssler Fiorenza,[9] while for research into *Ḥokmā* in the First Testament literature I want to give special mention to Claudia V. Camp, whose 1985 book *Wisdom and the Feminine in the Book of Proverbs*[10] served as a trailblazing contribution to critical feminist[11] study of personified *Ḥokmā*.

1. The Central Feminist-Theological Questions Surrounding the Phenomenon of Personified Wisdom

Feminist interest in *Ḥokmā* is, in the first instance, very concrete. Can this figure become the foundation for a new Christian spirituality? The answers are varied. For a few such as Susan Cady, Marian Ronan, and Hal Taussig[12] the positive aspects of the biblical bases for a contemporary *Sophia*-spirituality predominate; most, however, are skeptical, for they take *Ḥokmā* to be the tame reflection of the powerful ancient Near Eastern goddesses, and they suspect the androcentric texts of the Bible of not telling the whole truth about this figure—a suspicion that is not entirely unjustified.

In what follows I want to attempt to formulate the central feminist questions in a way that incorporates both the successful results and the problems of traditional historical-critical research.

1. To date traditional exegesis has not succeeded in reaching a consensus about the significance of *Ḥokmā*/*Sophia* in postexilic Israel. Is she a hypostasis,[13] a personified voice, the self-revelation of the mystery of creation,[14] or the redefinition of an Israelite goddess?[15] The central question appears to be still unresolved: What is the relationship between personified Wisdom and YHWH, the God of Israel? How does she fit into our picture of a monotheistic religion in the postexilic period?

2. In recent decades historical-critical exegesis has taken two different approaches to the phenomenon of *Sophia*, one religious-historical and the other Israel-internal.[16] While the religious-historical works have taken the female character of *Ḥokmā* seriously insofar as they investigated her variegated relationships with the image especially of Egyptian and Hellenistic goddesses,

all those who have attempted to understand Wisdom from within the Israelite tradition—with the exception of Bernhard Lang— scarcely took notice of her femaleness. However, it is insufficient to explain the female character of so central a figure by saying that *ḥkmh* is a feminine noun in Hebrew and the Hebrew language has a preference for female personifications. It is also insufficient to decipher the goddess-heritage of *Hokmā* without answering the question of what she meant for the people of Israel or how it was possible for such a goddess-like female symbol to push her way into the immediate proximity of YHWH. Claudia Camp articulates this second central question quite simply in the introduction to her study: "A book" (namely Proverbs) "*was* constructed with dominant female images and it *was* accepted into Israel's canon. Why?"[17]

Methodologically, what is particularly crucial for feminist exegesis is to move from the texts about personified Wisdom to their contexts. That means:

1. Personified Wisdom must be read in close connection with each of the Wisdom writings and her function within Proverbs, the Book of Job, etc., must be minutely examined, for especially in the book of Jesus Sirach she appears in an extraordinarily misogynist context, and in principle we must begin by supposing that she is a patriarchally-derived figure. On closer examination we also find that there is no such thing as personified Wisdom *per se,* but instead that *Hokmā/Sophia* has a very different character in the various Wisdom writings.

2. To move from the texts to the contexts also means methodologically that we must regard images of God not only as the expression of spiritual- or theological-historical developments, but also as a response to communal, social, political, cultural, and religious changes in a particular epoch.[18] It is not enough to establish that here and there *Hokmā* takes on a mediating role between the distant YHWH and the people. This phenomenon calls for explanation. Why does this mediating figure appear precisely in the image of a woman and precisely in the postexilic period, and what exactly does she mediate?

3. It is methodologically fruitless to approach the texts directly with theological questions such as the relationship between *Hokmā*

and monotheism. But if personified Wisdom appears and speaks as a woman, then a more thorough investigation of the connections between the image of women in the postexilic period (or in the Wisdom literature) and this image of God could prove revealing. As the discussion of the goddess or God image in Hosea has shown, in God-imagery central theological components always encounter anthropological elements.[19] The meaning of the word "woman" when personified as "Wisdom" is an essential key to its correct understanding. Only in this way will we find an explanation for why it was first in the postexilic period that the heritage of the ancient oriental goddesses was received in a non-polemical way, while these goddesses were demonized and suppressed in the majority of biblical literature before the exile.[20]

I want, then, to formulate the goal of feminist research into divine Wisdom as follows: Its aim is to reconstruct in a feminist-theological way the postexilic history of *Sophia* as an integrating component of Israel's theological history, and this, in turn, as an integrating part of the history of Israelite women.[21]

2. Women's Wisdom at the City Gates and the House of Wisdom

In what follows I will use images of women and images of God in the book of Proverbs to show how feminist exegesis deals methodologically with the texts and the questions posed above.

Personified *Hokmā* meets us in her most colorful and brilliant manifestation in Proverbs 1–9. Let us focus our attention first on the localities in which or from which Wisdom speaks, and second on some very interesting connections between these texts and the conclusion of the book in 31:10-31, the so-called "praise of the capable wife." The first entrance of *Hokmā,* her preaching of judgment and call to repentance directed to the simple and the stubborn, takes place before a significant backdrop:

> Wisdom cries out in the street;
>   in the squares she raises her voice.
> At the busiest corner she cries out;
>   at the entrance of the city gates she speaks (Prov 1:20-21).

In ch. 8 very similar scenery forms the background for the long speech of *Ḥokmā* to the men of Israel and the children of humanity:

> Does not wisdom call,
>> and does not understanding raise her voice?
> On the heights, beside the way,
>> at the crossroads she takes her stand;
> beside the gates in front of the town,
>> at the entrance of the portals she cries out . . . (Prov 8:1-3).

Despite the Hebrew text, the details of which present a number of problems,[22] this backdrop is not hard to interpret. *Ḥokmā* appears preaching or teaching in the public squares of the Israelite city, or, to put it simply, in public. The gate is the place of meeting and of assembly, where announcements are made, agreements are reached, justice is administered. According to Neh 8:3, Ezra reads the Torah from the square in front of the Water Gate. Whether instruction was also given at the gate is a question I will not go into.[23] Another image is introduced in Proverbs 9:

> Wisdom has built her house,
>> she has hewn her seven pillars.
> She has slaughtered her animals,
>>> she has mixed her wine,
>> she has also set her table.
> She has sent out her servant girls,
>>> she calls
>> from the highest places in the town,
> "You that are simple, turn in here!"
>> To those without sense she says,
> "Come, eat of my bread
>> and drink of the wine I have mixed!" (Prov 9:1-5).

Here the interpretation of the scene is somewhat more difficult. What kind of a house is it that Wisdom has built, and into which she invites—a palace, a luxurious dwelling, a temple?[24]

The work of Wisdom clearly unfolds in public and at home, the connection between which is established in ch. 9 by the servant girls sent out. If Wisdom appears here in the figure of a woman, then the following question suggests itself: What does it mean that a *female* figure appears at the city gates and there proclaims her teaching, that she can appear as house builder and host? What presuppositions must have been in place in the patriarchal Israelite environment that would have made her convincing as a personification in these roles and allowed her to find acceptance as a religious symbol? This situation gives special significance to the biblical "models" for a woman in these roles.[25]

Thus in Israel's literature women not only climb the city walls in order to slay an Abimelech with a millstone (2 Sam 11:21). The wise woman of Abel of Beth-maacah calls out from the city (*mn h'yr* 2 Sam 20:16) and summons Joab, the commander of David's army, because Joab wants to destroy a whole city with an ancient tradition of wisdom and counsel on account of a man who had taken refuge there. The LXX, both in 2 Sam 20:16 and in Prov 1:21, indicates more precisely the place from which the women speak than does the Masoretic text. It locates both women on top of the city wall: *ep' akrōn de teikheōn* and *ek tou teikhous*. The whole scene in 2 Samuel 20 shows similarities with Wisdom at the gates in the book of Proverbs. The woman's cry: "Listen! Listen!" is followed by a Wisdom discourse incorporating provocative questions. The woman of Abel not only bears the title "wise woman" (*'šh ḥkmh);* at the end of the passage it is again emphasized that she exhorted the whole population of the city "in her Wisdom" (*bḥkmth* 2 Sam 20:22; NRSV "the woman went to all the people with her wise plan"). Here we are presented with the image of a woman active in counseling, teaching, and prophecy, an image from Israel's literary history that prepared for Wisdom teaching at the gates or on the city walls and made her appearance there possible.[26]

In addition, the tradition of the First Testament knows women in the roles of household head, meal preparer, and host: Rahab of Jericho, who gave the spies lodging in her home (Joshua 2; 6:15-27); Jael, who lured Sisera into her tent (Judg 4:17-24); Tamar, who baked cakes for Amnon (2 Samuel 13); but also the woman from Shunem who had a small roof chamber with walls built and furnished for Elisha and accommodated him there (2 Kings 4:8-

17). When in Genesis 27 Rebecca prepares the meal with which Jacob obtains his father's blessing and when Esther (Esther 5–7) with her banquet prepares Haman's downfall, it is clear that women in the roles of meal preparer and host often bring about the most important decisions, even the decision over life and death.

Even more important than the literary-historical models for Proverbs 9 were the real historical models of women who built houses. After the return from exile women participated in model fashion in the rebuilding of houses and cities. In Neh 3:12 it is expressly mentioned that the daughters of Shallum took part in the rebuilding of the wall of Jerusalem; and according to Neh 5:1-5 it was the wives of the poor men who stood up for the preservation of their property and households, who protested against the debt-slavery of their sons and daughters, and who in every respect felt themselves just as responsible as the men.

Let us take another look at the concluding chapter of Proverbs, the praise of the strong or capable Israelite woman. Here again the text tells of a woman who is the head of her household:

> She rises while it is still night
> and provides food for her household
> and tasks for her servant girls (31:15).

> She is not afraid for her household when it snows,
> for all her household are clothed in crimson (31:21).

> She looks well to the ways of her household,
> and does not eat the bread of idleness (31:27).

Rightly has Pnina Navè Levinson emphasized that it does not suit the thrust of the poem to see in it the praise of a virtuous and diligent housewife, there for her family night and day, in accordance with the modern Christian-bourgeois marital ideal.[27] The *'št ḥyl* who is spoken about here is a wealthy woman who governs an entire household with the greatest economic and financial freedom —four times the text refers to *her* house—and the effects of her activity certainly do not stop at the house door, but extend to the poor and suffering (31:20) and also to her husband's public reputation (31:23), at the city gates.[28] Beyond this, what is astonishing in Prov 31:10-31 is not only the self-sufficiency of the *'št ḥyl*, but a significant number of comparisons and expressions in the text that leave no doubt that this woman is closely associated with God and divine Wisdom. Here I can indicate only a selection of the thematic connections that Hans-Peter Mathys more thoroughly investigated in his inaugural academic lecture.[29]

> A capable wife who can find?
>> She is far more precious than jewels (31:10).

The comparison with jewels and other valuable things is applied to *Ḥokmā* in three other places in the Wisdom literature:

> She is more precious than jewels,
>> and nothing you desire can compare with her (Prov 3:15).

> . . . for wisdom is better than jewels,
>> and all that you may desire cannot compare with her (Prov 8:11).

> No mention shall be made of coral or of crystal;
>> the price of wisdom is above pearls (Job 28:18).

The theme of finding also associates the wife with *Ḥokmā*. In Prov 18:22 we read:

> He who finds a good wife finds a good thing,
>> and obtains favor from the LORD.

In Prov 8:35 the same good fortune is associated with Wisdom:

> For whoever finds me finds life
>> and obtains favor from the LORD.

Like *Ḥokmā,* the strong woman has servant women or maids to whom she gives commands (Prov 9:3 and 31:15). She opens her mouth in wisdom and gives kind instruction (31:26). According to Prov 31:25 strength and dignity *('z-whdr)* are her garment. Who would not here be reminded of Ps 96:6 or 104:1, where it is said of God:

Honor and majesty are before him;
strength and beauty are in his sanctuary (96:6).

and

O LORD my God, you are very great.
You are clothed with honor and majesty (104:1).

In other respects as well, the praise and exaltation of the woman is unstinting in these verses:

Her children rise up and call her happy;
her husband too, and he praises her . . .
. . . a woman who fears the LORD is to be praised.
Give her a share in the fruit of her hands,
and let her works praise her in the city gates (31:28-31).

It is seldom that human beings are praised in the First Testament. In the overwhelming majority of cases God is the object of praise.[30] Also according to the consensus of the First Testament only God—and, in Prov 1:33, *Hokmā*—is legitimately deserving of trust *(bṭḥ)*.[31] But Prov 31:11 says:

The heart of her husband trusts *(bṭḥ)* in her [the wife],
and he will have no lack of gain *(šll)*.

The word "gain" (otherwise translated "booty"), somewhat odd in this context, alludes to Prov 1:13-14, which warns against the entice-ments of sinners who say: "we shall fill our houses with booty *(šll)*." Instead, one should follow Wisdom, with whom alone is certain "gain." When, then, we read at the very end of the poem that the woman's works proclaim her praise in the city gates, we should first of all think of *Hokmā,* who utters her own praise at the entrance to the city gates. Moreover, this expression and others remind us of the little book of Ruth.[32] After the night on the threshing-floor Boaz says to Ruth:

And now, my daughter, do not be afraid, I will do for you all that you
ask, for all the assembly of my people know that you are a worthy
woman *('št ḥyl)* (Ruth 3:11).

The LXX could not stand this extremely high evaluation and praise of the woman at the very end of the poem in Proverbs, and so drastically changes the text in Prov 31:28-31. It is not the *God-fearing* woman who should be praised, but the *intelligent* woman *(gynē gar synetē): she* shall praise the fear of YHWH, and finally it is not *she* who is to be praised at the gate, but *her husband.* The Hebrew text, in contrast, leaves no doubt at all that the capable woman represents *Ḥokmā* and, as her representative, deserves attributions that otherwise are reserved for YHWH alone.

If we return now to house-building Wisdom in the book of Proverbs it strikes us that the house-building power of Wisdom is also mentioned twice within the older collection of sayings in Proverbs 10–30. Thus in Prov 14:1:

> Wisdom of women *(ḥkmwt nšym)* has built her house,
>   but folly tears it down with her own hands.*

and in Prov 24:3:

> By wisdom *(bḥkmh)* a house is built,
>   and by understanding it is established;
> by knowledge the rooms are filled
>   with all precious and pleasant riches.

Obviously there is more at stake here than a house built of stones. This is about one's whole existence, about life in community. Wisdom invites into the house of life; those who follow folly into her house fall into Sheol and destroy their very existence (Prov 9:18). Amazingly, in Prov 14:1 and 24:3, the house-building power is once identified as *Ḥokmā* and once as the "wisdom of women."[33] Again the concrete wisdom of women is identical and interchangeable with personified *Ḥokmā,* just as the wisdom of the woman represents personified Wisdom in Proverbs 31. Conversely, *Ḥokmā* is not simply the personification of Wisdom, but instead personifies *women's* wisdom—the wisdom that would have given an Israelite woman her identity and acted as her life's security—in a special and significant way through the image of a woman.

The book of Ruth, whose time of composition would not be all that far from the framing parts of the book of Proverbs (around 450 B.C.E.), in a passage that, however, can with good reason be assigned to the secondary editing of the book in the second century B.C.E.,[34] clearly goes farther or says things *expressis verbis* that appear to underlie things said in the book of Proverbs. When the people and the elders say to Boaz (Ruth 4:11): "May the LORD make the woman who is coming into your house like Rachel and Leah, who together built up the house of Israel," Ruth's effect on the house of Boaz is made equivalent in significance to that of the two tribal ancestors who helped build the house of Israel, the existence and identity of Israel. What Ruth does in the house will establish a new community and a new life. So this woman is the image of a capable woman of the postexilic period who works for the rebuilding of Israel, for which, though a foreigner, she dedicates her life and applies her wisdom, and whose good reputation is known at the gates of the city.[35]

At this point I want to bring together these individual observations on the text and propose a thesis for interpreting them. It is apparent that personified *Ḥokmā* of Proverbs 1–9 and the capable woman of Proverbs 31 are related to each other, insofar as one of them is the woman "Wisdom" and the other is a wise woman. Both have house-building and -sustaining functions, both have public influence in different ways, the work of both of them has something to do with the fear of YHWH. Proverbs 14:1 directly confirms that the primary reference of personified Wisdom is the wisdom of women. The place of this woman-wisdom is in public as well as in the house, and the Israelite woman's work in the house gains her a place in public. Personified Wisdom is unthinkable without the "wise women" in the literature and history of Israel.[36] On the other hand, the work of a capable woman is seen as the working of *Ḥokmā* and one should not hesitate to praise and value her as one does divine Wisdom and even YHWH. YHWH can be experienced in the woman of Proverbs 31, and it is YHWH who speaks to Israel in personified *Ḥokmā* in Proverbs 1–9.

3. The Literary and Theological Function of the
Personification of Ḥokmā in the Book of Proverbs

To this point we have spoken of "personified" Wisdom, following the usual practice in most academic literature, without more
closely defining what this notion of "personification" implies.
However, an inquiry into the actual function of personification
yields some further insights into the literary shape of the book of
Proverbs and into the theological questions at hand. Behind the
text of Proverbs 1–9 is an implicit metaphor: "Wisdom is (like) a
woman who. . . ." This metaphor attempts to make something
that is incomprehensible and abstract into something more com-
prehensible, more concrete, and more familiar. The less-known
entity, the thing to be signified *[Signifikat]*, is "wisdom," which is
related analogously to the signifier *[Signifikant]* "woman." Thus
"woman" is an image of "wisdom." Personification, as a sub-category
of metaphor, is a style or a mode of expression that gives life to a
thing, that treats something not a person as if it were a person and
so links the abstract to the concrete; it personalizes the imper-
sonal. In its literary-poetic function personification emphasizes
the *unity* of the subject. From a multiplicity of women residents of
the city comes "Daughter Zion." At the same time personification
generalizes multiplicity. From the widest variety of manifestations
of human evils comes *"evil"*; from their many forms of stupidity
comes *"folly."*[37] Personification affects its readers only when it
stands within a tradition; otherwise it finds no acceptance. What
carries the most weight in affecting this acceptance is the predi-
cate, the signifier, to which we generally react in an unmediated
and emotional way—in this case the image "woman."

Claudia Camp has thoroughly demonstrated that "personified
Wisdom" as a stylistic device primarily assumes a unifying function in the overall redactional process of the book of Proverbs.[38]
The final redactor wanted to use ch. 9 and the conclusion of ch. 31
to frame the different Wisdom teachings in the collection of sayings. By means of personified Wisdom the teachings incorporated
in the sayings are unified into *the* Wisdom, into *one* teaching. So
Ḥokmā embodies the teaching tradition of the collection of
Proverbs and, beyond that, the Wisdom tradition of Israel. Thus

the right theological lens for reading the collected sayings is more or less furnished to readers of the book of Proverbs in the book's first nine chapters. I note in this connection the key suggestion of Fokkelien van Dijk-Hemmes and Athalya Brenner—which deserves serious attention—that Proverbs 1–9 does not transmit the teaching of a father to his son; instead, here a (fictional) mother speaks to her son.[39]

The choice of the stylistic device of personification in the framing chapters of the book of Proverbs has a theological significance as well. If it is true that by definition the purpose of personification is to join the abstract and the concrete, the question of whether and to what extent personified Wisdom is to be understood as a human or divine entity is falsely put. In itself this personification seeks to connect God and woman; its purpose is to connect the human, concrete, this-worldly with the divine, universal, and otherworldly, to connect Yhwh with the street, the house, love, the Wisdom tradition, and the life of Israelite women, so that the activities of the wise woman become transparent, even transcendent toward Yhwh, and Yhwh can be experienced in the image of "Lady" Wisdom. It is thus quite plausible that the plural construction *ḥkmwt* in Prov 1:20; 9:1; 14:1; 24:7; Ps 49:4; Sir 4:11; 32[35]:16 as a *pluralis intensitatis* may be a conscious parallel construction to *ʾlhym,* as has been proposed.[40] The plural also reminds us that divine Wisdom is closely connected with human forms of wisdom.

There is no need to explain in detail here that *Ḥokmā* in the context of the book of Proverbs is a divine figure, given the abundance of recent and past contributions on that topic. Her divine claim is revealed by the emphatic and weighty *ʾny* of the first person speeches, which calls to mind the self-presentation of Yhwh in Exodus 3 or in the Decalogue, but above all the Egyptian gods' self-presentations in their speeches.[41] From a form-critical perspective *Ḥokmā* speaks like a deity, or like the God of Israel.

Within the Israelite tradition Wisdom is also identified with Yhwh through the motif of seeking and finding, for example in Prov 8:17:

> I love those who love me,
>   and those who seek me diligently find me.

This motif is at home in love metaphors (Song 3:1-4), but also in prophetic texts, where it is applied to the relationship between YHWH and the people of Israel:

> With their flocks and herds they shall go
>   to seek the LORD,
> but they will not find him;
>   he has withdrawn from them (Hos 5:6; see also Amos 5:4-6;
>   Deut 4:29, and frequently elsewhere).[42]

Ḥokmā acquires still more of a kingly-godly image—though this originates outside Israel—when in Prov 8:14-16 she presents herself as patron of rulers and as the order according to which kings exercise their sovereignty.[43] But not only here is *Ḥokmā* drawn in the image of Egyptian Maat. The central text Prov 8:22-31, in order to speak of Wisdom's divine sovereignty, also borrows from Egyptian myths and Egyptian as well as Syrian goddess-iconography, something Othmar Keel and Urs Winter have demonstrated in detail.[44] This important text about *Ḥokmā* at the very beginning of creation leaves no doubt that she is a divine figure. She is not a created work, but rather was present before all created things and is an authoritative participant in the creation of the world. The text leaves her origins in the dark inasmuch as it twice says that YHWH "created me/set me up *(qnny),*" but then immediately, in relation to the twice-repeated "I was born/brought forth" *(ḥllty)* leaves open from whom and how.[45] In the context of the whole of ch. 8 it seems to me most reasonable to take seriously what vv. 22-31 say, recognizing that they do not *want* to define the relationship between YHWH and *Ḥokmā*. They can only explain this relationship narratively to the extent that, as regards her origin, Wisdom stands in close relationship to YHWH; that she was already there before creation; and that her vital power was active in creation. A vivacious young woman—not a child[46]—makes of creation a work arising out of cultic laughing and joking, and out of relationship. Hence it would be false, keeping in mind the whole context of ch. 8, to impute to these texts the notion that Wisdom here is *subordinate* to YHWH. The text avoids any statement that could be read as a clear expression of subordination. *Ḥokmā* is a counterpart for

YHWH, a divine counterpart. But she is not a child, not a daughter, not a goddess next to YHWH, nor is she a mediating hypostasis that divinizes *one* aspect of this God. *Ḥokmā* is the God of Israel in the image of a woman and in the language of the goddesses.

Proverbs 8:22-31 completely avoids the disastrous image of marriage with which Hosea had first relegated the female aspect in Israel's image of God to the second rank, to the advantage of the national god YHWH.[47] These verses do not envision a marriage partnership between YHWH and *Ḥokmā*. Instead, in the images in Proverbs 1–9 the feminine is associated in a new and creative way with transcendence and heaven, and what had become problematic over a period of centuries is rethought and experienced here for the first time: Transcendence is not only feminine, but also erotic, and all this *within* the Israelite religious symbol system.

I want to go one step farther here. In my opinion there is no basis for saying that there was an ancient Israelite Wisdom goddess before *Ḥokmā* who is now tamed in Proverbs and shut up in the cage of a completely closed monotheism with an exclusive character closed to any female expression.[48] We do not find the slightest indication that *Ḥokmā* became personified before the exile. Nothing points to the idea that this figure in Proverbs was deformed by specific patriarchal interests. Bernhard Lang's hypothesis rests on what I think is a questionable observation, namely that earlier mythical personifications are made into poetic personifications through rational reflection. There is no rule in place here, and that kind of reasoning from effect to cause is problematic because the more "naïve" mythical personifications have only been transmitted to us in poetic form, and because demonstrably there are some personifications that are purely poetic creations with no mythical "ancestors."[49] There is something to be said for the idea that the personified Wisdom of Proverbs is actually to be attributed to the final redactor of these collected texts. Nevertheless, *Ḥokmā* is a figure with a past, for her images also reflect to a considerable degree those of the Egyptian goddesses (Maat, Hathor, the consort of the gods), possibly also those of Syria. In many of her aspects the goddesses are visible and vivid. In the personification of Wisdom the heritage of the goddesses is taken up and thus integrated in reflective mythology, without any polemical intent.[50]

The Song of Solomon also demonstrates skillful, free, and imaginative treatment of the old mythical images and the vital power of the cult of the goddesses.[51] The circles of the older Wisdom poets were already familiar with this ancient Near Eastern heritage and had no inhibitions about giving expression to it.

Personified *Ḥokmā* is no attack on the ancient Israelite conviction—never fundamentally questioned in the Wisdom tradition—that YHWH is the God of Israel. Nor do we find any attack on the belief, explicitly formulated since the exile, that absolutely no other gods exist beside YHWH. The writers appear not to have regarded it as in any way necessary to defend a "correct" monotheistic idea of *Ḥokmā*. Personified Wisdom is instead the completely non-polemical attempt to set a feminine image of God in place of and alongside a masculine image, linking the God of Israel to the experience and the lives especially of the women in Israel, the Most High God to the realm of household religion, and beyond that to the images and roles of the ancient Near Eastern goddesses. To ask about the relationship of *Ḥokmā* to postexilic monotheism is thus somewhat misleading. It could be misunderstood to imply that this monotheism was already something theoretically and practically perfected, fixed on an exclusively masculine image of God, when Wisdom appeared. In fact, however, personified *Ḥokmā* is a Wisdom contribution to the development of early postexilic monotheism, a variety of monotheism that could take liberties with the patriarchal images of God and was able without inhibition to integrate the goddesses, even with their erotic aspects. Unfortunately this theologically unique and still unattained variety of monotheism did not gain any great historical success in Israel.[52]

4. *Image of Woman—Image of God—Monotheism. Points of Contact for a Feminist-Theological Reconstruction of the Historical and Religious-Historical Backgrounds*

Although I am aware that the following remarks pose more questions and hypotheses for future feminist studies than they offer clear answers, it is still important to me to locate the Wisdom image of God in the book of Proverbs within the larger historical and theological contexts of the early postexilic period and, beyond that, to attempt a quick look at the further destiny of this feminine image of God.[53]

For the men and women of Israel the exile meant the complete collapse of their national and religious identity. The land was taken from them, but so was the Temple, their house of worship and the symbol of YHWH's presence in the land. The monarchy, too, which had served the function of a sacral mediating instance between YHWH and Israel, was gone. Israel's religious symbol system was destroyed, and the people experienced the full, terrifying force of chaos. Hence it is not surprising that so many postexilic texts return repeatedly to the theme of creation in their profound need to assure themselves, in a period of chaos, of the existence of a still-standing or newly-expected order.[54] The theological reactions to the shock of exile were many-layered and very different, as different as the groups, movements, and classes from which they came. Even after the return of the exiles a great deal was in flux, and every new development had to be theologically assimilated.

One thing among many that had changed was the world of women and thus also the image of women. According to an ancient rule it appears that the position of women in a society actually improves in times of crisis or war.[55] There are some indications of this, as well as that the catastrophe of the exile and the miserable new beginning changed the role and the perceptions of women in Israel. It is possibly not altogether accidental that it was precisely in the period of exile that the Priestly document produced the insight that men and women are made in the image of God. Above all, the rebuilding and the struggle to survive were also concerns of women. Naomi and Ruth had to survive that struggle, and they acquired a home, land, and family. The new life that begins for Job after the time of crisis also means that his daughters receive a name and even a portion of inheritance among their brothers (Job 42:13-15).[56] The changed position of women in this time may be grammatically reflected in the postexilic texts in that feminine forms of nouns and verbs appear to be used more frequently. Thus the constant shifts in gender in the second and third chapters of the book of Ruth almost remind one of the contemporary efforts to achieve inclusive language.[57] Deutero-Isaiah, but also Ezra and

Nehemiah, make frequent explicit mention of daughters along with sons, and women along with men, etc. (See Isa 43:6 and Neh 8:3.)

We cannot fail to see that women are accorded recognition in religious matters, that they appear as religious subjects, and not only in private, inside their homes, but also in the public realm and on the level of popular religion. Thus in Prov 1:8 and 6:20 the father's instruction and the mother's teaching are mentioned in the same breath.[58] Women thus took over the transmission of the religious tradition, the "teaching" of Torah. A whole biblical book, Ruth, treats the theme of the solidarity of women, but also the faith of two women. Prophets like Noadiah (see Neh 6:14) involve themselves deeply in the political-religious events of the day; the wife of a man like Job (see Job 2:9-10) appears as the spokeswoman for a theological position. Ezra is explicitly said to read the Law before men and women (Neh 8:1-3; 10:29-30). Deutero-Isaiah (Isa 51:2) reminds the people not only of Abraham, but also of Sarah, "who bore you."

In the exilic and early postexilic period house and family become not only the sustaining social unit, the only one that could assure survival and indeed the only one that was still functioning; in the new religious symbol system they became the place where Israel could experience YHWH, where religious identity could constitute itself anew. The house took over some of the functions of Temple and monarchy. This had radical consequences, because the cult of the national god, YHWH, which had been centralized in Temple and palace throughout the period of the monarchy, was now suddenly transferred entirely to the sphere of home and family, where before the exile this national God was in no way at home. As in the pre-national period, recalled, for example, in the stories of Ruth or Job, in reaction to the altered social-religious relationships images of God changed and became more familial.[59] God is Redeemer and Father (Ruth; Isa 63:16-17; Mal 2:10), but also consoling Mother (Isa 49:15; 66:13), or else a woman in labor pains (Isa 42:14). But there may have been resistance precisely on the part of women against YHWH's seizure of the religious sphere of household and family. Jeremiah 44, the prophet's accusation against the women and men in exile in Egypt concerning the worship of YHWH or of the Queen of Heaven (see Jer 7:16-20), is a very informative text, for it shows that the most fundamental and radical challenges to the value and meaning of YHWH-worship came from the milieu of family, where the national God played a very minor role, while from the Queen of Heaven one could expect bread, security, peace, and prosperity.[60] It is within these areas of tension that we should locate the different theological currents of the early postexilic period.

The message and praxis of the Deutero- and Trito-Isaian movements are completely in line with the new experience of God: that God is a God of the poor, who loves just acts more than false piety in service of the exploitation of one's own people (e.g., Isaiah 58). The theology of these students of Isaiah is sustained by an integrative universalism pointing beyond Israel that dares to understand someone like Cyrus as YHWH's messiah (Isaiah 45), that assures foreigners and eunuchs of full participation in God's salvation (Isaiah 56), that includes the whole creation and all peoples in the new history of God with Israel. This God, according to Isa 57:15, is enthroned "in the high and holy place, and also with those who are contrite and humble in spirit."

Deutero-Isaiah has little interest in the Temple as the dwelling place of God or in the cultic life and priesthood associated with the Temple. Trito-Isaiah even expresses a very critical view of the Temple in light of its planned restoration:

Thus says the LORD:
Heaven is my throne
    and the earth is my footstool;
what is the house that you would build for me,
    and what is my resting place? (Isa 66:1).

If there is to be a Temple at all, then it is to be a house of prayer for all peoples (Isa 56:7); if there are to be priests at all, then those who suffer and those who mourn shall be called priests of YHWH (Isa 61:6). For Deutero- and Trito-Isaiah faith in the God YHWH who can be known in world history and in creation fundamentally precludes the existence of other gods, but not speaking about YHWH in female-motherly images. The monotheism of these movements is patriarchal, but not in the sense of establishing a front against women or female images of God as such.[61]

Those also who are at home in the circles of the Wisdom tradition, toward whom Deutero-Isaiah adopts a somewhat skeptical stance (see Isa 44:25), seek answers to the challenges of the time; they want to "seek and find God." Proverbs 1–9, but also Job (ch. 24) describe reality after the return from exile very much as Trito-Isaiah does (e.g., in Isaiah 57). Exploitation and injustice rage among the people, one person depriving another of existence, and in one and the same family there are rich and poor. Proverbs probably directs its appeals more strongly to the group of potential exploiters, the well-to-do people of a cultured upper class. They are warned:

> . . . if sinners entice you,
>   do not consent.
> If they say, "Come with us, let us lie in wait for blood;
>   let us wantonly ambush the innocent . . ." (Prov 1:10-11)

or:

> Do not withhold good from those to whom it is due,
>   when it is in your power to do it.
> Do not say to your neighbor, "Go, and come again,
>   tomorrow I will give it"—when you have it with you.
> Do not plan harm against your neighbor
>   who lives trustingly beside you (Prov 3:27-29).

Proverbs 1–9; 31:10-31, rooted in the old logic of the relationship of actions to consequences, aspires in its new form to a condition of solidarity in Israel, *ṣdqh*. No longer is the king endowed with wisdom the guarantor of the divinely-approved order, but Wisdom herself is the guarantor, God in the image of the woman preaching conversion, who is also rebuilding the house of Israel; of women who stretch out their hands to the suffering and the poor (Prov 31:20); or, like the foreign mother of Lemuel, admonish their sons to intercede in favor of justice for widows and orphans, for the suffering and the poor (Prov 31:8-9). Wisdom takes over the classic functions of the Israelite kings (revealer of the will of

God, guarantor of an order and justice pleasing to God, representative of the rule of YHWH, authoritative counselor).[62]

The appeals of *Ḥokmā* are urgent and beseeching, argumenta-
tive, but helpless. Wisdom threatens and promises; she puts herself in the balance against every kind of capital and every spoil
(Prov 8:10-11, 18-19), and predicts that those who depart from
solidarity will only injure themselves; she accuses them of necrophilia (Prov 8:36). The frame of the book of Proverbs breathes the
same spirit of universalism and border-defying internationalism as
Deutero- and Trito-Isaiah, but it goes a decisive step further in
constructing an independent female image of God. *Ḥokmā* is an
inviting and integrating symbol. This theology needs Zion and the
Temple as little as does Trito-Isaiah.

The role the "strange woman" plays in this new Wisdom theology and the concrete reality the texts about the "strange woman"
are reacting against are matters difficult to clarify. There are no
reasons to believe that the "strange woman" or the "foolish woman"
in Proverbs were conceived as personifications, but as religious
symbols they incarnate the opposite of *Ḥokmā*, namely the endan-
gering of identity rather than its finding, death instead of life.[63] But
in Proverbs the center of interest is not this figure as such; it is
men's adultery and the fact that they have abandoned the wives of
their youth. Ezra, in contrast (Ezra 9–10; Nehemiah 13) reacts
with fanatical and ultimately, it would appear, futile laws against
mixed marriages by requiring that all foreign wives be driven out.
Ezra, like Malachi (see Mal 2:16), can appeal to the ancient Israelite suspicion of the daughters of a strange god. The Book of Ruth
responds to this xenophobia and sexist attitude with the story of a
Moabite woman who becomes a model follower of YHWH. Ruth's
conduct at the threshing floor is not so different from that of the
"strange woman" of Proverbs. But this text attempts to awaken
solidarity toward foreign women and thus to oppose misogynism.

Concern for a more open and integrative YHWH-faith in which
women would be taken more seriously as religious subjects and in
which the religion of YHWH would be related more closely to family life and thus also to the lives of women came to a swift end in
the restoration. Zerubbabel and Jeshua, supported by Haggai and
Zechariah, pressed for the reconstruction of the altar and the

Temple in Jerusalem. Ezra drove away the foreign women and took measures for the exact observance of the Law (1 Esdr 9:1-10, 44; Neh 8:1-8). Nehemiah pressed forward with the building of the city wall. Resistance to this restoration movement (see, for example, Ezra 4:1-23), in which women were clearly participants (Noadiah in Neh 6:14), had little success. After a short time a new alliance of Temple, Law, and priesthood took shape; it became the leading movement in the postexilic period and was increasingly able to theologically curb the other, independent traditions in Israel, including the Wisdom tradition. This development of a renewed Temple- and cult-centered religion, dominated by the Zadokite priests and shaped by priestly notions of purity, had grave consequences for women as well as for the Wisdom image of God. The hierocratic and theocratic model is inimical to women, at least in its consequences.[64] One symbol of this misogynism is the seventh vision of Zechariah, in which the woman in the basket (*ephah*) is banished from the land. A house is to be built for her in Shinar, where she is to stay, for there is no house for her in Israel (Zech 5:5-11).[65]

5. The Fate of Divine Wisdom in the Later Wisdom Literature

Each of the Wisdom writings of the later period in which personified *Hokmā* appears has its own image of women and of God, and thus mirrors both the images of women and of God in its own time and those of the redactor or of the circle in which the redactor moved. In principle, it appears to be possible to demonstrate a correlation between personified Wisdom and the understanding of Wisdom in the respective texts. Moreover, there is also a correspondence between the Wisdom image of God and the image of women.

We find that, except in Sirach 24, Wisdom no longer approaches or speaks to Israel in the first person. Even *Hokmā* in Job 28 is, in comparison to the multiplicity of her aspects in Proverbs 1–9, a pale figure hidden from human beings and accessible only to God, a heavenly-cosmic figure representing the order of the world. But then, astonishingly enough, in the second century B.C.E. Jesus ben Sira uses Wisdom to shape the central theological chapter, the pivot point of his book.[66] Even though with Jesus Sirach *Ḥokmā* recovers more color and is even fitted with new imagery,[67] my study of the texts tends to indicate that the author has placed personified Wisdom in the service of a thoroughly patriarchal theology. Even the scope of the texts about good and bad wives, daughters in need of paternal control, and many other feminine dangers[68] makes us suspect that Ben Sira considered women a "primary topic" and dedicated himself to this theme with some pastoral interest. Women in Israel have apparently not become as submissive as he wants them to be. His texts do not so much reflect the overall state of things as they project masculine desires.[69] What Jesus Sirach understands as women's wisdom is that a wife honors her husband (26:26), that she obeys and supports him (36:29), that she exerts herself so that he may grow old in peace, and that she is always silent (26:1-2, 14). "Do not give yourself to a woman and let her trample down your strength" (Sir 9:2): With such and similarly pointed statements the author strengthens the patriarchal power of men in Israel.

He also uses theological weapons in his battle here, for the submission of the feminine to the masculine is again clearly portrayed in his Wisdom image of God. Thus the programmatic first chapter emphatically develops the title verse "All wisdom is from the Lord," a statement with a very exclusive claim.[70] According to Ben Sira only God is wise, and wisdom consists solely in fear of God (Sir 1:14-30). Such reflections are not new, having a place also in Proverbs (2:6 and elsewhere). What is new, however, is the insistence on the close connection between wisdom and fear of God. Chapter 24, which portrays Sophia in the garments of the tree goddesses of Palestine and Egypt, then binds this figure unmistakably to the people of Israel, to Jerusalem, and to service in the Temple. Finally, in a further development of the union of Law and Wisdom already accomplished in Deut 4:5-6, she is identified with the Torah of Moses (an absolutely decisive turning point for Jewish religion).[71] Jesus Sirach, who unites in his own person a priest learned in Scripture and a Wisdom teacher, makes *Ḥokmā* a kind of hypostasized representative of the "Wisdom of the Lord," a priestly mediatrix in Temple service. Wisdom does not invite into *her* house, but into the Temple, and she enters the workrooms of the Scripture scholars as a motherly-sisterly beloved.[72] For Jesus Sirach monotheism is exclusively patriarchal. The femaleness of *Ḥokmā* here takes a clearly subordinate position; her relationship to YHWH and her sphere of operations are clearly delimited. She obediently takes the place YHWH chooses for her (Sir 24:8).

The Wisdom of Solomon contains a highly conflicted image of Wisdom. On the one hand, no other First Testament writing goes so far in erotic language, describing the relationship between God and Sophia as one of intimate love and depicting Sophia as sitting beside God *(paredros)*.[73] The Sophia of the Wisdom of Solomon seems also to have been affected in the first century B.C.E. by the (extraordinarily emancipatory) theology of the religion of Isis, as John S. Kloppenborg has shown in a convincing article.[74] On the other hand, now only a select few, an elite, can ask God for Wisdom or experience her in intensive study. The Sophia of chs. 6–9 has a remote and heavenly-spiritualized air.[75]

As for the groups responsible for the book of Wisdom, perhaps we should consider communities like the men and women *Therapeutes* in Philo's *De vita contemplativa*. This group lived apart from the turmoil of the cities and led an ascetical-spiritual life devoted entirely to the study of the Scripture, nourished literally on Wisdom as their food *(De vita contemplativa* § 35). Women were also admitted into community; they lived and studied by themselves but were in no way discriminated against in the cultic table fellowship.[76] However, the price of the equal privilege and individual dignity that the book of Wisdom also grants to women (Wis 3:13; 4:1-2) ought to make contemporary women skeptical. Spiritualization, hatred of the body, and consolation in the life to come are a heritage that has been especially influential in Christianity.

Philo of Alexandria is proof that the broad use of Wisdom as a female image of God did not decline in the centuries before and after the turn of the era. In one enormous acrobatic act he accomplishes the feat of making Wisdom male and calling her "Father":

> And [in this passage] he calls Bethuel the father of Rebekkah. How, then, can the daughter of God, namely, wisdom, be properly called a father? is it because the name indeed of wisdom is feminine but the sex masculine? For indeed all the virtues bear the names of women,

but have the powers and actions of full-grown men, since whatever is subsequent to God, even if it be the most ancient of all other things, still has only the second place when compared with that omnipotent Being, and appears not so much masculine as feminine, in accordance with its likeness to the other creatures; for as the male always has the precedence, the female falls short, and is inferior in rank. We say, therefore, without paying any attention to the difference here existing in the names, that wisdom, the daughter of good, is both male and a father, and that it is that which sows the seeds of, and which begets learning in, souls, and also education, and knowledge, and prudence, all honourable and praiseworthy things.[77]

There is no other explanation for these abstruse speculations than that Philo was reacting to groups and opinions that took the femaleness of Sophia literally.[78] His philosophical-theological speculation aims at attributing the original, biblical attributes of Sophia to the masculine Logos and making Sophia a mother figure, the mother of the Logos.[79] Although the influence of Philo already makes itself very sensibly felt in the writings of the Second Testament—which prefer to speak of *pneuma* and *logos* rather than *sophia*—we can still reconstruct, from the gospels to the letters, a vital continuing life of the Wisdom image of God as well as the development of a *Sophia* christology. Elisabeth Schüssler Fiorenza[80] has demonstrated that it was just this God- and Christ-imagery that gave decisive emancipatory impulses to early Christianity and lent theological support to the integrative and open praxis of table fellowship with those who in that time were commonly excluded. Despite this revival, however, the church fathers of the first four centuries of Church history succeeded in excluding biblical Sophia once again, and in preventing her from assuming the place she should have had among the people or in trinitarian thought. Christian iconography of Sophia, but also the texts of someone like Hildegard of Bingen, show nonetheless that efforts to break the female power of this figure were never completely successful.[81]

6. Sophia: The Future of a Feminist Christian Spirituality

If we may take it as a starting point that we will not regard the figure of personified Wisdom as obsolete, and that we choose to

remove it from its First Testament wrappings in a form appropriate for current consumption, I want to give an energetically af-
firmative answer to the question of whether Wisdom can be the
future of a Christian feminist spirituality. As basis for such a spirituality preference should be given, on feminist theological
grounds, to the *Ḥokmā* of Proverbs. What historically justifies us
and should also empower us in bringing the biblical text's Wisdom image of God back into our contemporary theology and
Church life is above all the similarity of the exilic and postexilic
epochs to the challenges of our contemporary world. The old images of women are crumbling, just as are the purely masculine images of God. The Church is faced with a decision: in light of all
the new challenges of this era will it attempt a restoration, or does
it have the courage to cross boundaries, to break down walls instead of rebuilding them? *Ḥokmā* could make many contributions
to a more integrative, more open Christian religion.[82]

1. *Ḥokmā* can be developed as an equal-ranking female image
of God, interchangeable with the male God-image, standing alongside and, at the same time, critically correcting that image without
calling monotheism into question. In addition, there is a biblical
tradition that identifies her with Christ, who is neither male nor
female. And within the Trinity Sophia can alternatively assume
the place of the Holy Spirit.

2. Personified Wisdom integrates the Ancient Near Eastern and
Hellenistic goddesses in reflective mythology; indeed, she takes
her life from the language, the images, the theology, and the
power of the veneration of Maat, of Hathor, and of Isis. Here
would be an opportunity (and I am thinking not only of the god-
dess-seeking women of Europe, but also of the Hindu-Christian
dialogue in India) to shape the Jewish-Christian religion and tradition into a real home for women.

3. Personified Wisdom is a figure who creates connections and
connectedness. She joins transcendence to the female, God to
human experience, theology to everyday reality, the woman teacher
to the teaching, the creatrix to the principle of creation. Sophia
spirituality will serve the solidarity of human beings with one another and of human beings with creation; out of her own inner
power she will cross over the boundaries of cultures, of nations,

and of races, the boundaries between poor and rich, man and woman, and the boundaries between the religions. She could contribute to making our theology have more to do with the world, and to causing the world to pay more attention to the needs of women and the voice of God.

It is this integrating power that makes *Ḥokmā* one very promising future for Christian spirituality, though perhaps not the only one. In this way our contemporary images of God could be enriched through the richness of the biblical images of God. For "you shall not make for yourself an image of God"—so Jewish theologian Marcia Falk translates and updates the commandment against making images[83]—does not mean "you shall not make for yourself *any* image of God," but "you shall not make for yourself only *one* image of God." For *one* image of God is the image of an idol.

NOTES

[*] Since the first appearance of this article a great lacuna in the research mentioned in it has been filled by the outstanding work of Christl Maier in exegesis and social history. In her monograph this author investigates with painstaking care the meaning of the "strange [or "loose"] woman" of Proverbs 1–9, and in this connection also takes up her counterfigure, personified *Ḥokmā*. She demonstrates conclusively that in the province of Judea in the late Persian period such warnings against the "strange woman" were used to integrate young men of the Judean upper classes into the tried and true patriarchal family order. Contact with women outside one's relational boundaries constitutes a danger to a respectable and successful life, while a sexual relationship outside marriage is simply out of the question. According to Maier, *Ḥokmā,* as a positive figure with whom to identify, serves to bind women also within this patriarchal system, and the figure of the "foolish woman" serves as a negative image. If *Ḥokmā* in the book of Proverbs were basically nothing but a function of a patriarchal social order designed by the upper class and unfavorable to women, naturally a great shadow would fall on this figure from a feminist point of view. However, under this presupposition it is impossible to explain why Wisdom in Proverbs 1–9 never appears as a motherly figure, which would have been the desired feminine role *par excellence.* It seems probable that in fact the image of *Ḥokmā* goes beyond the traditional

roles in many aspects and should therefore also be evaluated as a constructive and "modern" reaction to the changing situation and images of women.

My rather negative estimation of the Wisdom of Solomon (briefly summarized on p. 38 above) has changed as a result of my intensive reexamination of the contexts of that book, as the detailed study of personified *Sophia* in the book of Wisdom in Chapter 7 of this volume shows. The impression that the text is elitist and tends to spiritualization is not corroborated by a closer reading. Only a longer period of work with the text opened my eyes to its exciting implications for an intercultural theology.

Newer literature:

Gerlinde Baumann, "Gottes Geist und Gottes Weisheit, Eine Verknüpfnung," in Hedwig Jahnow, et al., *Feministische Hermeneutik und Erstes Testament. Analysen und Interpretationen* (Stuttgart: Kohlhammer, 1994) 138–48 examines the connection between *ruaḥ* and Wisdom.

Athalya Brenner, ed., *A Feminist Companion to Wisdom Literature,* Feminist Companion to the Bible 9 (Sheffield: Sheffield Academic Press, 1995) contains a variety of contributions on women's roles in the Wisdom books and a number of articles on the "strange" woman. The entire book is stimulating; in addition, it contains a comprehensive bibliography.

Christl Maier, *Die "fremde Frau" in Proverbien 1–9. Eine exegetische und sozial-geschichtliche Studie.* OBO 144 (Fribourg: Universitätsverlag; Göttingen: Vandenhoeck & Ruprecht, 1995) has detailed further references to literature on this theme.

1. Susan Cady, Marian Ronan, and Hal Taussig, *Sophia: The Future of Feminist Spirituality* (San Francisco: Harper & Row, 1986).

2. Elisabeth Moltmann-Wendell, *Das Land wo Milch und Honig fließt. Perspektiven einer feministischen Theologie* (Gütersloh: Gerd Mohn, 1985) 103ff. (English: *A Land Flowing with Milk and Honey: Perspectives on Feminist Theology.* Translated by John Bowden [New York: Crossroad, 1986] 91–102.)

3. Rosemary Radford Ruether, *Sexism and God-Talk* (Boston: Beacon, 1983) 54–61.

4. For a historical-critical study of the meaning of *rwḥ* see Helen Schüngel-Straumann, *Ruaḥ bewegt die Welt. Gottes schöpferische Lebenskraft in der Krisenzeit des Exils.* SBS 151 (Stuttgart: Katholisches Bibelwerk, 1992). See also, by the same author, "Ruaḥ" in M. Kassel, ed.,

Feministische Theologie. Perspektiven zur Orientierung (Stuttgart: Kohlhammer, 1988) 59–73 (with further bibliographic references for *rwḥ*).

5. See Moltmann-Wendell, *A Land Flowing with Milk and Honey* 97.

6. Elisabeth Schüssler Fiorenza, *In Memory of Her. A Feminist Theological Reconstruction of Christian Origins* (New York: Crossroad, 1983) 133.

7. Rosemary Radford Ruether, *Sexism and God-Talk* 57. Gerda Weiler also writes very skeptically about biblical Wisdom. See her *Ich brauche die Göttin. Zur Kulturgeschichte eines Symbols* (Basel: Mond-Buch, 1990) 140.

8. Let me mention Dieter Georgi, "Frau Weisheit oder Das Recht auf Freiheit als schöpferische Kraft" in Leonore Siegele-Wenschkewitz, ed., *Verdrängte Vergangenheit, die uns bedrängt. Feministische Theologie in der Verantwortung für die Geschichte* (Munich: Kaiser, 1988) 243–76, and two studies of mine published as chapters 9 and 10 in this volume.

9. See n. 6 above. Compare also the little book by Deirdre J. Good, *Reconstructing the Tradition of Sophia in Gnostic Literature.* SBL.MS 32 (Atlanta: Scholars, 1987).

10. Claudia V. Camp, *Wisdom and the Feminine in the Book of Proverbs* (Decatur, Ga.: Almond, 1985). See also her "Woman Wisdom as a Root Metaphor. A Theological Consideration," in Kenneth G. Hoglund et al., eds., *The Listening Heart: Essays in Wisdom and the Psalms In Honor of Roland E. Murphy,* JSOT.SS 58 (Sheffield: JSOT Press, 1987) 45–76. A somewhat older publication works with archetypal categories: Joan Chamberlain Engelsman, *The Feminine Dimension of the Divine* (Philadelphia: Westminster, 1979).

11. I use the term "critical feminist" in the sense used by Schüssler Fiorenza. (See *In Memory of Her* 1–95.) See also her *Bread Not Stone: The Challenge of Feminist Biblical Interpretation* (Boston: Beacon, 1984). The term implies the demands of the historical-critical method and a feminist option.

12. *Sophia* passim.

13. Othmar Keel gives a brief overview of the contributions to the discussion about hypostasis. See his *Die Weisheit spielt vor Gott. Ein ikonographischer Beitrag zur Deutung der mᵉṣaḥāqät in Sprüche 8,30f.* (Fribourg: Universitätsverlag; Göttingen: Vandenhoeck & Ruprecht, 1974) 12–13.

14. This is the view of Gerhard von Rad in his *Weisheit in Israel* (3rd ed. Neukirchen-Vluyn: Neukirchener Verlag, 1985) 189–204. (English: *Wisdom in Israel* [Nashville: Abingdon, 1972] 144–76.)

15. Thus Bernhard Lang in *Wisdom and the Book of Proverbs. A Hebrew Goddess Redefined* (New York: Pilgrim, 1986).

16. In what follows I can only refer in the most summary fashion to the foundational revisions in scholarship made by Claudia Camp. See her *Wisdom and the Feminine* 21–68 and 149–78.

17. Ibid. 17.

18. Many contributions to the social-historical exegesis of the "crisis of Wisdom" in the postexilic period appear to me of special methodological importance in this connection: Rainer Albertz, "Der sozialgeschichtliche Hintergrund des Hiobbuches und der 'Babylonischen Theodizee,'" in Jörg Jeremias and Lothar Perlitt, eds., *Die Botschaft und die Boten, Festschrift für H. W. Wolff* (Neukirchen-Vluyn: Neukirchener Verlag, 1981) 349–72; Frank Crüsemann, "Die unveränderbare Welt. Überlegungen zur 'Krise der Weisheit' beim Prediger (Kohelet)," in Willy Schottroff and Wolfgang Stegemann, eds., *Der Gott der kleinen Leute. Sozialgeschichtliche Bibelauslegungen, I: Altes Testament* (Munich: 1979) 80–104 (English: "The Unchangeable World: The 'Crisis of Wisdom' in Koheleth," in *God of the Lowly: Socio-Historical Interpretations of the Bible.* Translated by Matthew J. O'Connell [Maryknoll, N.Y.: Orbis, 1984] 57–77); idem, "Hiob und Kohelet. Ein Beitrag zum Verständnis des Hiobbuches," in Rainer Albertz et al., eds., *Werden und Wirken des Alten Testaments, Festschrift für Claus Westermann* (Göttingen: Vandenhoeck & Ruprecht; Neukirchen-Vluyn: Neukirchener Verlag, 1980) 373–93.

19. See Marie-Theres Wacker, "Frau—Sexus—Macht. Eine feministisch-theologische Relecture des Hoseabuches," in eadem, ed., *Der Gott der Männer und die Frauen.* Theologie zur Zeit 2 (Düsseldorf: Patmos, 1987).

20. For the demonization of the goddess see above all the study of Urs Winter, *Frau und Göttin. Exegetische und ikonographische Studien zum weiblichen Gottesbild im Alten Israel und in dessen Umwelt.* OBO 53 (Fribourg: Universitätsverlag; Göttingen: Vandenhoeck & Ruprecht, 1983).

21. The proposal for a history of Israelite religion in which Israelite women appear as subjects is also strongly emphasized by Phyllis Bird, "The Place of Women in the Israelite Cultus," in Patrick D. Miller, Jr., Paul D. Hanson, and S. Dean McBride, eds., *Ancient Israelite Religion: Essays in Honor of Frank Moore Cross* (Philadelphia: Fortress, 1987) 397–419.

22. See Otto Plöger, *Sprüche Salomos.* BKAT XVII (Neukirchen-Vluyn: Neukirchener Verlag, 1984) 11–21, 84–88.

23. Bernhard Lang, *Wisdom and the Book of Proverbs* 22–33, has made the idea that school instruction took place at the gate a mainstay of his proposal that *Ḥokmā* was a "school-goddess" or "goddess of writing." To this point, however, neither First Testament texts nor archaeology has offered any proof of his thesis. (On this see Horst Dietrich Preuß, *Ein-führung in die alttestamentliche Weisheitsliteratur* [Stuttgart: Kohlham-mer, 1987] 45–46.) Among others things, the question arises why, if something like teaching took place at the city gate, the First Testament so frequently refers to justice being administered at the gate but never refers to a school in that location. I think Lang confines the figure of *Ḥokmā* too narrowly to her role as teacher. Her claim that the decision over life and death falls to her is a prophetic claim, not a pedagogical one.

24. See the discussion in Plöger, *Sprüche Salomos* 99–104, and Lang, *Wisdom and the Book of Proverbs* 90–96.

25. The question of literary-historical models is methodologically im-portant and is characteristic of the work of Claudia Camp. Compare what follows also to my essay on "Wise Women," Chapter 3 of the present vol-ume.

26. On the "wise woman" see especially Claudia Camp, *Wisdom and the Feminine* 120–23.

27. Pnina Navè Levinson, *Was wurde aus Saras Töchtern? Frauen im Judentum* (Gütersloh. Gerd Mohn, 1989) 29.

28. In an older story Abigail lays claim to a similar radius of activity (1 Samuel 25). However, her idea of a reasonable economy (including the payment of taxes) seems to coincide less fully with that of her spouse than is the case in Proverbs 31. See Silvia Schroer, "Abigail: A Wise Woman Works for Peace," Chapter 5 in this volume.

29. For what follows I am indebted to Hans-Peter Mathys, unpublished manuscript of a lecture on Prov 31:10-31.

30. See Claus Westermann, *"hll," THAT* 1:494.

31. Erhard S. Gerstenberger, *"bṭh," THAT* 1:303–305.

32. Here I cannot go into the many minor details that link the strong Ruth and her husband Boaz to Prov 31:10-31. Let me only indicate that the praise of Judith is also proclaimed from the city gate of Bethulia (Jdt 13:17-20). A woman's virtue and integrity are judged at the gate. At the same time, a woman like Tamar (see Gen 38:14) can provoke judgment and sentence on others by going to the city gate.

33. It is true that the Masoretic text vocalizes *ḥakᵉmōt nāšīm*, ("wise women"), but the rest of the verse is clearly singular in form *(bnth byth)*. (Thus the NRSV gives "The wise woman builds her house" with the mar-

ginal note "Heb *Wisdom of women*". –Tr.) On this see Plöger, *Sprüche Salomos* 166–67, and further below on the meaning of plurals.

34. On this see Erich Zenger, *Das Buch Ruth*. ZBK.AT 8 (Zürich: Theologischer Verlag Zürich, 1986) 93.

35. Women's strength in building up houses is also expressed in 1 Sam 25:28, where Abigail promises David: "the LORD will certainly make my lord a sure house." In Ps 144:12b the daughters of Israel are likened to "corner pillars, cut for the building of a palace." One may speculate whether pillars in the form of women are to be imagined here and whether there is some significance to the idea of architecture in the sense of "house-supporting" women. Frequently temple plans show two women or goddesses in place of stylized palmettos or similar architectural ornaments. For example, see Siegfried Mittmann et al., eds., *Der Königsweg, 9000 Jahre Kunst und Kultur in Jordanien*. Exhibit Catalogue (Mainz: P. von Zabern, 1987) no. 128; Amihai Mazar, "Pottery Plaques Depicting Goddesses Standing in Temple Facades," *Michmanim* 2 (1985) 5–18.

36. Camp demonstrates this in her *Wisdom and the Feminine*, 79–147.

37. On the function of the metaphor see Othmar Keel, "Zeichen und Zeichensysteme" (unpublished manuscript). On the function of personification see Ethelbert W. Bullinger, *Figures of Speech Used in the Bible* (Grand Rapids: Baker Book House, 1975) 861ff.

38. Camp, *Wisdom and the Feminine* 209–25.

39. "On Gendering Biblical Texts," a paper prepared for the International Meeting of the Society of Biblical Literature in Vienna in 1990. I received the paper in manuscript after this essay was finished, and so I was unable to incorporate all its important aspects here.

40. On the possible meanings of these plurals see Plöger, *Sprüche Salomos* 13.

41. See Christa Bauer-Kayatz, *Studien zu Proverbien 1–9. Eine form- und motivgeschichtliche Untersuchung unter Einbeziehung ägyptischen Vergleichsmaterials*. WMANT 22 (Neukirchen-Vluyn: Neukirchener Verlag, 1966) 75–95. On p. 85 the author refines the comparison of YHWH-speeches in first-person style with the first-person speeches of *Ḥokmā*, because the formal differences are great. See the contribution of Gottfried Vanoni, "Göttliche Weisheit und der nachexilische Monotheismus. Bemerkungen und Rückfragen zum Beitrag von Silvia Schroer," in Marie-Theres Wacker and Erich Zenger, eds., *Der eine Gott und die Göttin*. QD 153 (Freiburg: Herder, 1991) 183–90.

42. For particularities on these metaphorical expressions see Gillis Gerleman, *bqš, THAT* 1:333–36; 922–25. Marie-Theres Wacker briefly

addresses the special significance of seeking and finding in Hos 5:6 in her essay, "Frau—Sexus—Macht," (n. 19 above) 118 n. 50. It could have been a reference to a mythologically-based rite of seeking and finding (the deceased god).

43. See Bernhard Lang, *Wisdom and the Book of Proverbs* 60–70.

44. Keel, *Die Weisheit spielt vor Gott* (n. 13 above), and Winter, *Frau und Göttin* (n. 20 above) 516–23. See also Silvia Schroer, "Die Zweiggöttin in Palästina/Israel. Von der Mittelbronze-Zeit IIB bis zu Jesus Sirach," in Max Küchler and Christoph Uehlinger, eds., *Jerusalem: Texte, Bilder, Steine.* NTOA 6 (Fribourg: Universitätsverlag; Göttingen: Vandenhoeck & Ruprecht, 1987) 218–21.

45. Here I am basing what I say on the conclusions of the detailed exegesis by Othmar Keel in *Die Weisheit spielt vor Gott* 9–30.

46. The uncertain *ʾāmôn* in the Hebrew text of Prov 8:30 has given support to many very patriarchal speculations. However, in *Die Weisheit spielt vor Gott* (21–30) Othmar Keel has already given some strong arguments against the "pampered child" interpretation; he argues in favor of a young woman active in cultic life who entertains YHWH with her jokes. The mythic and iconographic backgrounds for this joking Wisdom come above all from Egypt (Maat, Hathor, playful divine consorts), but the life-loving goddesses of the old Syrian cylinder seals appear also to have influenced Israelite Wisdom in these texts. See Keel, *Die Weisheit spielt vor Gott* 31–68, and Winter, *Frau und Göttin* 516–23.

47. On this see Marie-Theres Wacker, "Frau—Sexus—Macht," passim. YHWH is related to the people and the land of Israel as a patriarchal husband and master instead of a goddess who had "seduced" them from YHWH. The female entity is firmly fixed in a subordinate position within the hierarchical order.

48. This is the major thesis of Bernhard Lang's book, *Wisdom and the Book of Proverbs.*

49. On personification see Lang, *Wisdom and the Book of Proverbs* 132–36. As an example of a personification without any mythical basis let me point to the Greek Tyche. (See Herbert Hunger, *Lexikon der griechischen und römischen Mythologie* [6th ed. Hamburg: Rowohlt, 1974] 415–16.) Nike was unknown to Homer, while in Hesiod she emerges as the personification of victory, the gift of Zeus or Athene. In the Greek cult she played almost no role at all. (See Hunger, *Lexikon* 272.) Lang's reference (p. 131) to *Aram. Ach. Pap.* 54.1 can scarcely be counted as an indication of personified Wisdom outside Israel or Judaism, since the subject of the verses is only inferred from the context and the text leaves so many questions open. On this see Max Küchler,

Frühjüdische Weisheitstraditionen. Zum Fortgang weisheitlichen Denkens im Bereich des frühjüdischen Jahweglaubens. OBO 26 (Fribourg: Universitätsverlag; Göttingen: Vandenhoeck & Ruprecht, 1979) 46, 388.

50. On this conceptualization see Schüssler Fiorenza, *In Memory of Her* 133. It should be noted that all written mythology in Israel is "reflective mythology."

51. See Othmar Keel, *Das Hohelied* (Zürich: Theologischer Verlag Zürich, 1986). The goddesses do not appear to be purely poetic in the Song of Solomon either, as for example the adjuration of the love goddess "by the gazelles or the wild does" (Song 2:7) shows. See ibid. 91–94.

52. I would like to insert here a few ideas I find important, arising out of the discussion after the presentation of the lecture on which this chapter is based. The un-folding *[Ent-faltung]* of the monotheistic image of God into a male and female person in relationship to each other is a highly interesting step in the history of theology. Jewish theology (cf. the "Ancient of Days" and the "Son of Man" in the book of Daniel), and then above all the Christian doctrine of the Trinity have sought the one God in a twofold or threefold expression, but ultimately by suppressing the female image of God. Behind this attempt at un-folding the one God may be the recognition that a monolithic and static image of God conceals dangers within itself and that even a "single" god can only be described in personal categories of relationship.

53. Claudia Camp has elucidated some of the social-historical, political, and cultural aspects of the Wisdom image of God in the fourth part of her book, *Wisdom and the Feminine,* at pp. 227–82. Building on her work, I am attempting to establish still further possible connections, most of all with other texts and currents of thought in the postexilic period.

54. On this see Paul D. Hanson, "Israelite Religion in the Early Post-Exilic Period," in Patrick D. Miller et al., eds., *Ancient Israelite Religion* 485–508.

55. This seems to be the case even though at the same time pauperization affects women and children above all.

56. In connection with daughters' right to inherit, Num 27:1-11 and 36:1-12 on the daughters of Zelophehad ought to be more thoroughly researched. See the article by Ebernard Bons, "Erbe, Erben," in Manfred Görg and Bernhard Lang, eds., *Neues Bibel-Lexikon* (Zürich: Benziger, 1988–) 4:555–58.

57. On the gender shifts in postexilic language see the brief references in Erich Zenger, *Ruth* 27, 53. In any case there has not yet been a plausible explanation for this grammatical peculiarity in Ruth 2–3. But see

Gottfried Vanoni's article in Wacker and Zenger, eds., *Der eine Gott und die Göttin* 183–96.

58. According to Deut 4:10; 11:19-20 parents are responsible for the religious education of children.

59. On this see Erhard S. Gerstenberger, *Jahwe, ein patriarchaler Gott?: traditionelles Gottesbild und feministische Theologie* (Stuttgart: Kohlhammer, 1988) 17–27.

60. See Gerstenberger, *Jahwe* 27–37. For the cult of the Queen of Heaven see also Winter, *Frau und Göttin* 455–60, 561–76.

61. Gerstenberger, *Jahwe* 26.

62. Claudia Camp, *Wisdom and the Feminine* 272–75. See also my essay "Wise Women," Chapter 3 in this volume.

63. That the "woman of foolishness" is a personification is no longer generally accepted. See Plöger, *Sprüche Salomos* 106–109. The history of reception has made the "strange woman" a symbol of the demonic and evil (cf. 4Q184, 13). On this see especially Max Küchler, *Schweigen, Schmuck und Schleier. Drei neutestamentliche Vorschriften zur Verdrängung der Frauen auf dem Hintergrund einer frauenfeindlichen Exegese des Alten Testaments in antiken Judentum.* NTOA 1 (Fribourg: Universitätsverlag; Göttingen: Vandenhoeck & Ruprecht, 1986) 192–209. The results of Claudia Camp's research on the "strange woman" are still somewhat unsatisfying, in that she is not completely able to explain the juxtaposition of the woman-friendly figure of Wisdom and the woman-hating figure of the "strange woman." See Camp, *Wisdom and the Feminine* 136–37, 265–71.

64. It is a concern of mine not to lend support to the old—sometimes starkly anti-Jewish—clichés about the restoration as a comprehensive cause and agent of all developments that are unpopular today. Whether the theocratic symbol system is misogynist by definition must be very closely scrutinized historically, by Jewish women theologians as well. A differentiated and cautious presentation of the restorationist groups in their confrontation with other postexilic movements and theologies is hence very desirable. The contribution of Phyllis Bird *(The Place of Women in the Israelite Cultus)* appears to me to be too little guarded methodologically against the continual threat of Antisemitism, which occurs also in Christian scholarship regarding women. On this, see Leonore Siegele-Wenschkewitz, ed., *Verdrängte Vergangenheit* (n. 8 above).

65. In 1994 Christoph Uehlinger published a thorough analysis and explanation of the vision of the woman in the basket, in which he uses iconographic material, among other things, to demonstrate that this text signifies a program for the final expulsion of the goddesses from Judah.

See his "Die Frau im Efa (Sirach 5.5-11). Eine Programmvision von der Abschiebung der Göttin," *BiKi* 49 (1994) 93–103.

66. Personified *Ḥokmā* appears in Sirach 1; 6:18-31; 14:20–15:10; 24; 51:13-20. On this see my essay "The One Lord and Masculine Domination in the Book of Jesus ben Sirach," Chapter 6 of the present book.

67. Thus Sir 14:20–15:10 and especially Sirach 24 know *Ḥokmā* in the form of the tree- or branch-goddess, whom the author may have known from Palestinian and Egyptian traditions. On this point see my essay, "Zweiggöttin," (n. 44 above) 218–21.

68. There are indications of the author's attitude toward women in Sir 3:2-16; 4:10; 6:1; 7:19-27; 9:1-9; 19:2; 22:4-5; 23:16-27; 25:1, 8, 13-26, 27; 28:14; 33:20; 35:17-18; 36:23-27; 37:11; 41:20-22; 42:6-14; 47:19-20.

69. On this methodologically important starting point of critical-feminist exegesis see Schüssler Fiorenza, *In Memory of Her* 56–60. Androcentric texts—Schüssler Fiorenza uses the Mishnah as an example —should not be taken as objective presentations of historical reality. They should instead be suspected of being "socio-theological projection[s] of men" (ibid. 58), that is, constructions of reality in reaction to the socio-political currents of their time. If an androcentric text strongly stresses the subjection of women to patriarchal domination, this is more an indication that this subjection was disputed than a portrayal of the norm. Warren C. Trenchard comes up short in his study, *Ben Sira's View of Women, a Literary Analysis* (Chico: Scholars, 1982) when he looks only for personal reasons for Ben Sira's hatred of women.

70. This exclusive claim could be directed against Hellenistic philosophy or against non-Israelite religions. It could also be aimed at currents within Judaism itself for which personified Wisdom had attained an independent significance as a female image of God.

71. Let me refer here to the research of Max Küchler, *Frühjüdische Weisheitstraditionen* (n. 49 above) and Eckhard J. Schnabel, *Law and Wisdom from Ben Sira to Paul: a tradition-historical enquiry into the relation of law, wisdom, and ethics.* WUNT 2nd ser. 16 (Tübingen: J.C.B. Mohr [Paul Siebeck], 1985).

72. Furthermore, it is Jesus Sirach who first brings *Ḥokmā* into connection with the role of mother. See Sir 15:12 and possibly 24:18.

73. See Wis 8:3-4; 9:4. The many erotically colored words in the Greek texts have been mostly "watered down" in the translations of the Bible in general circulation (see Dieter Georgi, *Weisheit Salomos. Jüdische Schriften aus hellenistich-römischer Zeit* 3/4 [Gütersloh: Gerd Mohn, 1980] 429–30 [and see his note 2a]). On the book of Wisdom compare Georgi's essays, "Frau Weisheit" (n. 3 above) and "Zum Wesen der

Weisheit nach der 'Weisheit Salomonis,'" in Jacob Taubes, ed., *Gnosis und Politik*. Religionstheorie und Politische Theologie 2 (Munich and Paderborn: W. Fink, 1984) 66–81.

74. John S. Kloppenborg, "Isis and Sophia in the Book of Wisdom," *HThR* 75 (1982) 57–84.

75. See my since-revised estimation of this text in the postscript that follows immediately after the main text of this essay, marked with an *.

76. On the women *Therapeutes* see Dieter Georgi, "Frau Weisheit," 249–53.

77. *De fuga et inventione* §51-52 (on Gen 25:20). Translation from C. D. Yonge, translator, *The Works of Philo. Complete and Unabridged* (new updated ed. Peabody, Mass.: Hendrickson, 1993) 325.

78. See the discussion of this text by Dieter Georgi, "Frau Weisheit," 249–53.

79. See the monograph by Burton L. Mack, *Logos und Sophia. Untersuchungen zur Weisheitstheologie im hellenistischen Judentum.* StUNT 10 (Göttingen: Vandenhoeck & Ruprecht, 1973).

80. *In Memory of Her* 130–40; eadem, "Auf den Spuren der Weisheit —Weisheitstheologisches Urgestein," in Verena Wodtke, ed., *Auf den Spuren der Weisheit: Sophia, Wegweiserin für ein weibliches Gottesbild* (Freiburg: Herder, 1991) 24–40. See also Gottfried Schimanowski, *Weisheit und Messias. die jüdischen Voraussetzungen der urchristlichen Präexistenzchristologie.* WUNT 2nd ser. 17 (Tübingen: J.C.B. Mohr [Paul Siebeck] 1985), and Karl-Josef Kuschel, *Geboren vor aller Zeit? Der Streit um Christi Ursprung* (Munich and Zürich: Piper, 1990) (English: *Born before all time?: the dispute over Christ's origin* [London: SCM Press, 1992]).

81. See the article by Monika Liesch-Kiesl, "'Sophia' in der bildenden Kunst," *Bibel heute* 103 (1990) 158–60.

82. The following points are a summary depending on Cady, et al., *Sophia* 76–93.

83. Marcia Falk, "Toward a Feminist Jewish Reconstruction of Monotheism," *Tikkun* 4/4 (1989) 52–56.

CHAPTER THREE

Wise Women and Counselors in Israel: Prototypes for Personified *Ḥokmā*

1. Personified Wisdom: Foundation for a New Spirituality?

As a statement of a radical feminist critique of the Judeo-Christian image of God, Mary Daly's now-famous dictum, "if God is male, then the male is God," hits the nail on the head. A great many Christian women in the United States and in Europe are no longer content with minor reforms of the liturgy and half-hearted cosmetic changes to this dominant male God-image.[1] For some time now there has been a groundswell of voices among women who, despite everything, do not want to make a complete break with the Judeo-Christian tradition, and who see in biblical Wisdom a still-hidden potential for a new feminist Christian spirituality. Their primary interest in Israelite Wisdom thus originates in the fact that personified *Ḥokmā* is the sole recognized female divine image in Israel—although appearing first after the exile—and that this figure undoubtedly absorbed elements of ancient Near Eastern goddess cults. *Ḥokmā* bears unmistakable features of Egyptian Maat, of the lively love-goddess Hathor, and of the erotic Syrian goddess (see especially Proverbs 8); she is the heir of the Palestinian bough goddesses and the Egyptian tree goddesses (see especially Sirach 24), and in Alexandria she became a religious symbol that constituted a striking theological link between Israelite and Jewish traditions and the cult of Isis (see the book of Wisdom).[2]

Of course the mere fact that Wisdom is pictured as a woman or a goddess is not an adequate theological criterion. One must understand the significance of this religious symbol in the context of the postexilic period. Only on the basis of such a historical inquiry can we make a solid judgment of whether Sophia can represent the future of feminist spirituality. For the most part this feminist-critical work to establish the suitability of the Sophia theology of the First Testament for this purpose has not yet been done. *Ḥokmā* comes to us in writings that are clearly androcentric in character, and in part are unmistakably misogynistic (the latter is especially true of Jesus Sirach). She appears in the book of Proverbs alongside a powerfully demonic contrasting female figure, the "strange woman." Moreover, the whole of biblical Wisdom literature should probably be attributed to educated and therefore upper-class groups within Judaism. Add to this that it is not immediately apparent from the biblical texts whether Sophia is to be understood and revered as a being subjected to YHWH or as a primary religious symbol in place of YHWH. What we know of this background requires that we not greet Wisdom too hastily as a new symbol of the divine at the end of the twentieth century. In what follows I would like to offer a small contribution to feminist critical exegesis by tracing one of the roles of personified *Ḥokmā* to its place in the literature and life of ancient Israel: namely, the role of Wisdom as wise woman and counselor.

2. Wisdom as Counselor

In the books of Proverbs, Sirach, and Wisdom of Solomon personified Wisdom appears in a variety of roles, images, and symbols. Thus *Ḥokmā* is at the same time God's creation, his co-creator, and the principle that permeates creation, the principle of world order. She is God's lover, seated beside him on his throne, and she is the beloved, the wife, and the sister of the student of Wisdom. She is a host who sends servants into the streets to invite others to a meal in her house. She is a protecting and nourishing tree goddess who gladdens the student of Wisdom with her fruits. She is a wrathful teacher and preacher who raises her voice in the streets, and she is the counselor of kings and sages. In Prov 8:12, 14-16 Wisdom sings her own praises:

> I, wisdom, live with prudence,
>> and I attain knowledge and discretion. . . .
> I have good advice *('ṣh)* and sound wisdom;
>> I have insight, I have strength.
> by me kings reign,
>> and rulers decree what is just;
> by me rulers rule,
>> and nobles, all who govern rightly.

And in Wis 8:9 King Solomon, the patron of Wisdom, reports:

> Therefore I determined to take her to live with me,
> knowing that she would give me good counsel
> and encouragement in cares and grief.

In these texts the connection of counseling Wisdom to kings, rulers, and nobles is prominent. The close union of Wisdom and counsel, however, can be found in many other sayings in the Wisdom literature:

> My child, be attentive to my wisdom;
>> incline your ear to my understanding,
> so that you may hold on to prudence,
>> and your lips may guard knowledge (Prov 5:1-2).

> Fools think their own way is right,
>> but the wise listen to advice (Prov 12:15).

> Listen to advice and accept instruction,
>> that you may gain wisdom for the future (Prov 19:20).

Ḥokmā frequently complains that her advice is thrown to the wind and is not accepted (Prov 1:25, 30), and in the book of Wisdom we read that God's counsel cannot be known without Wisdom, the holy spirit from on high (Wis 9:17). Of course the teaching and counseling functions of Wisdom frequently overlap, which may well lie in the nature of the thing.

The next question should be why it was the female *Ḥokmā* in particular who assumed the role of counselor in Israelite Wisdom literature. In the first place, in the Egyptian texts that influenced or served as models for these, the king/father hands on practical teachings to his son; that is, the counselor in the literary fiction is normally a man. In addition, the position of counselor at the royal court in Israel was apparently reserved for men. How did it happen that female *Ḥokmā* appeared in the role of counselor to the powerful? It would seem that in this case the prototypes and models for this identification must not be sought solely in the history of religion outside Israel. Let me say unequivocally that I have no intention of denying the godmother-role of the Egyptian goddess Maat for Wisdom, including Wisdom as counselor, the Wisdom who, in Proverbs 8, evidently appears also as a leader and patron of the ruler. Without any doubt there are influences from the Ancient Near East with regard to this role as well; those cultures contain a whole series of goddesses who function as royal patrons, as Bernhard Lang, among others, has pointed out.[3]

However, there are also reasons internal to Israel for the development of the image of counseling Wisdom, namely the remarkably stable historical and literary tradition of counseling women in Israel, a subject first intensively researched by Claudia Camp.[4] There was a basis within Israel for Wisdom's assuming particular features and roles of the goddesses. Let us turn to that now.

3. Women as Counselors in Israel

A variety of types of counseling women appear in the First Testament, namely "wise" women, wives who give advice, and mothers who counsel their children.

Wise Women as Counselors[5]

Besides women prophets, the First Testament tradition is aware of "wise" women who, in crucial situations, intervene diplomatically in politics and decisively influence the course of things by their counsel. In 2 Samuel 14 Joab has a wise woman from Tekoa brought to King David to convince him, by means of a stratagem, that he should not banish his son Absalom. Her procedure is similar to that of the prophet Nathan, who uses a parable to bring David to recognize his own unjust behavior (2 Samuel 12).

Another woman who is called "a wise woman" stops Joab from massive bloodshed at the siege of Abel of Beth-maacah by negotiating with him from the city wall. In both cases "wise woman" seems to describe a status or office, and apparently the influence of these women was considerable. They are masters of the art of diplomacy; interestingly enough, both of these women appeal to Wisdom traditions.[6] The woman from Tekoa reminds David: "We must all die; we are like water spilled on the ground, which cannot be gathered up. But God will not take away a life; he will devise plans so as not to keep an outcast banished forever from his presence" (2 Sam 14:14; cf. Ps 22:15).

The wise woman from Abel of Beth-maacah refers to her city's leading role as a place of advice and counsel in Israel. Both women's advice is given for the sake of the life of an individual or a community. I would also bring Abigail in 1 Samuel 25 into company with these two figures; it is true that she is not expressly called "wise," but she is said to have "good sense" and thereby is made a figure of contrast to her husband Nabal ("Fool"). Abigail also intervenes with diplomatic skill, applying brilliant rhetoric and appealing to the God of Israel to prevent unnecessary bloodshed and preserve the lives of her household. At the same time she preserves the future king from blood-guilt.[7]

Judith, who has sufficient reputation to be able to summon the elders of her city, and whose wisdom is duly praised by those same men (Jdt 8:29) is also a "wise" woman. The book of Judith can be accounted a unique illustration of the image of women in the first century B.C.E.[8] At a time of great peril the heroine comes to the rescue of Israel, entirely with feminine means, but in the knowledge that she is leading a new Exodus of Israel in accordance with YHWH's will.

Wives as Advisors

Besides these wise women, who were even summoned before kings and whose counsel was highly prized, the First Testament contains a large number of wives who give advice to their spouses. Claudia Camp has rightly pointed out that in Israel the wife's advisory function was the most important of her tasks besides her role in the house.[9] Although the transitions between advice and action are sometimes slippery, the following examples leave no doubt that women are depicted as counselors: Abraham listens to Sarah's advice that he should beget an heir with the slave woman Hagar (Gen 16:2). Rebekah advises Isaac to send Jacob to Mesopotamia to seek a wife (Gen 27:42–28:9). Michal counsels and helps David to flee from Saul (1 Sam 19:11). Bathsheba succeeds in persuading David that it is right that he should make Solomon the heir to his throne (1 Kings 1). Solomon is "counseled" by his foreign wives in cultic matters (1 Kings 11:1-8). Jezebel advises Ahab not to give up on obtaining Naboth's vineyard (1 Kings 21). The great woman of Shunem counsels her husband to build a roof chamber for the prophet Elisha (2 Kings 4). Job's wife advises him in his misery that he should curse God and die (Job 2:9). In the book of Esther, Zeresh, the wife of Haman, is counted among his advisors (Esth 6:13). What all these women have in common is their success: there is scarcely a single case (except that of Job) in which the man does not listen to his wife, whether her advice is for good or ill.

The Wisdom books are also aware of the value of a clever and understanding wife who stands at her husband's side with advice and counsel. This is especially true of Proverbs (31:10, 26). It is striking how the wife is paralleled with *Ḥokmā* in various metaphors in Proverbs. Both Wisdom (Prov 3:15; 8:11; Job 28:18) and the capable wife (Prov 31:10) are more precious than jewels. Both Wisdom (Prov 4:8-9) and the good wife (Prov 12:4) are a garland or a crown for the wise, just as are the counsel and advice of one's parents (Prov 1:8). Whoever finds a wife obtains favor from YHWH (Prov 18:22), as does one who finds Wisdom (Prov 8:35). A prudent wife is from YHWH, as is Wisdom (Prov 19:14; cf. Sir 1:1). The reputation and praise of the capable wife (Prov 31:31; cf. Ruth 3:11) resound in the gates of the city, like the reputation of hidden Wisdom (cf. Job 28:21) or the loud cries of *Ḥokmā* as she goes about among the people (Prov 1:21; 8:3).

This interchangeability of wife and *Ḥokmā* in metaphorical usage is, I think, an indication that the (wise) wife was in fact regarded and experienced as the representative or incarnation of Sophia. In the Wisdom of Solomon the counselor Sophia is described as Solomon's bride and life companion, and at the same time as the lover and spouse of God (Wisdom 7–9). Unfortunately, the translations in general use conceal the genuinely erotic terminology in the Greek so much that one can scarcely sense anything of this love affair.[10]

We also find these erotic comparisons of Wisdom with the wife of one's youth, the life partner, in Jesus Sirach. The tenor of that book, however, as far as women are concerned, is fundamentally different from that of Proverbs and the Wisdom of Solomon. Here, in Sirach, beauty frequently ranks before intelligence, and a woman's intelligence consists primarily in silence and respect for her husband. The value of a woman is now almost exclusively regarded as capital for her husband. There are no women among the man's good advisors in Sir 37:7-18; on the contrary, a man is advised not to consult with his principal wife in matters concerning his concubine.[11]

The King's Mother as Advisor and the Mothers of the Nation

In addition to the wise women and clever wives there is a third literary model for *Hokmā,* namely mothers as counselors. In Proverbs the mother is almost always mentioned together with the father as the one who gives "counsel" to her children. Her role as maternal advisor apparently brought the mother of the king in Judah special honors, political authority, and major influence.

It is true that we know very little directly from the First Testament texts about the office of the *gebira,* the queen mother or female counselor to the king.[12] In light of some recent contributions,[13] however, the following may be regarded as certain:

1. This was a political office normally occupied by the birth mother of the reigning king. According to Jer 13:18 (cf. 29:2) in Judah both the king and the *gebira* wore crowns.

2. This institution was unique to Judah, since in the northern kingdom only the Phoenician princess Jezebel was referred to (by the princes of Judah) with this title (2 Kings 10:13).

3. The story of the deposition of the *gebira* Maacah by her son Asa (1 Kings 15:9-14) suggests that the cult of Asherah was under the special protection of the queen mother.[14]

4. One of the *gebira*'s principal duties was giving (political) advice to the king.

The last can be clearly detected in the story of Bathsheba, who, at Adonijah's request, attempts to persuade her son Solomon to give Abishag the Shunammite to Adonijah as his wife (1 Kings 2:13-23). He relies entirely on the queen mother's influence with her son: "'Please ask King Solomon—he will not refuse you . . .'" (1 Kings 2:17). The king receives his mother: he rises to meet her and bows before her in *proskynesis,* and he has a throne for her placed at his right hand. Although he at first promises to do as his mother requests, he instead has Adonijah executed.

We find a further indication of the influence of the *gebira* as counselor in 2 Chron 22:2-4, where the note about Ahaziah is expanded by a crucial sentence not found in 2 Kings 8.27:

2 Ahaziah was forty-two years old when he began to reign; he reigned one year in Jerusalem. His mother's name was Athaliah, a granddaughter of Omri.

3 He also walked in the ways of the house of Ahab, *for his mother was his counselor in doing wickedly.*

4 He did what was evil in the sight of the LORD, as the house of Ahab had done; for after the death of his father they were his counselors, to his ruin.

Probably in Dan 5:10-12 the reference is also to the queen mother, who advises the terrified King Belshazzar to call on Daniel to interpret the mysterious writing on the wall. Finally, in a puzzling chapter in the book of Proverbs we find the maternal advisor of the king once again, namely in the speech of Lemuel, the king of Massa (Prov 31:1-9). Although the addressee of this counsel and its localization remain a mystery, there can be no doubt that here advice is being given to the king by his mother. She counsels him to reticence in his dealings with women and abstemiousness in the use of alcohol. She even advises him, in the sense of an ideal kingship, to exercise his duties as a righteous judge, the defender of widows, orphans, and the poor, and not to neglect them.[15]

Other indications of the close connection between the maternal role and the counseling function in political contexts were assembled by Pieter A. H. deBoer in his outstanding and deeply inspiring 1955 essay, "The Counsellor."[16] His close inspection of the terms "counsel," "give counsel," and "counselor" in the Hebrew texts led him to the conclusion that not only do counsel and wisdom belong inseparably together, but the counsel of a specially authorized person in Israel was regarded as an oracular, life-ensuring decision valid for the life of the individual and for the people as a whole.

Prophetically gifted counselors were probably called "Father" or "Mother" in Israel. Thus according to Gen 45:8 Joseph became a "father" to Pharaoh, that is, his counselor. Joash, the king of Israel, called Elisha "my father" (2 Kings 13:14; cf. 2 Kings 2:12). One of the titles of the ideal king in Isa 9:6 is *ʾbjʿd,* which deBoer translates "counselor for the future." Correspondingly, Deborah is called "mother in Israel" in Judg 5:7. DeBoer's interpretation,[17] that this title emphasizes her role of counselor for Israel as one determinative of the future, is more persuasive than the usual interpretations of the phrase as a title of honor. Deborah is, after all, presented in Judg 4:4-5 as a wise judge and prophet who counsels the people in crucial situations and offers her own aid in carrying out the plan. And when, in the story of the wise woman in Abel of Beth-maacah mentioned above, the city is praised as a "mother in Israel," this must mean that Abel of Beth-maacah was a city of good counsel, a famed locus of oracles, or a place where wisdom, including the wisdom of women, was cultivated.

4. Women Counselors in Israel: Literary and
Historical Prototypes for Wisdom as Counselor

As the result of this inquiry let us conclude first of all as follows: Although the profession of counselor in the narrower sense of an official at the royal court may have been entirely reserved to men, counseling and "wisdom" in Israel was by no means a male domain. In private or in the political sphere, women had influence over their patriarchal environment. Prophetically gifted women, wives, and mothers were entitled to exercise that influence through their counsel, and to translate it into deeds. The high authority of a woman as counselor was apparently not limited by status or class. The narratives take place both in the royal courts and throughout the land. The social ubiquity of the "counselor woman" is connected with the continuity of this "type" of woman. The sources confirm this for the whole time period from the early days of Israel to the postexilic years.

That personified Wisdom appears as a female counselor is therefore something that can be established from evidence within Israel, that is, it is founded on socio-cultural factors within Israel's tradition and history. The literary figures of women in the First Testament must, of course, be seen as exceptional, but they certainly embody the ordinary experiences of the people of their time as well. The prototypes for counseling *Ḥokmā* are like these historically important women with unusual public authority. I am using the concept of a "prototype" in the sense of a shaping model that is significant in terms of its effects, not in the sense of a literary dependence on individual First Testament stories. The literary and historical counseling women in Israel made it possible for personified Wisdom to appear in that role or for religious-historical influences to be received. Wise women, wifely advisors, and mothers in Israel appealed for centuries to *Ḥokmā* and to her wisdom, and they were recognized as representatives of *Ḥokmā*.

Hence an essential element in the image of women, but also the authentic experience and identity of women in Israel may be integrated into the female image of God of the postexilic period through personified Wisdom as counselor. Sophia, who in a variety of images represents the gracious and humane side of the God of Israel, thus in all probability offered women of that time opportunities for identification, and it may be that this image of God had retroactive influence on the esteem accorded to women and on their social reality.

5. *The Socio-Religious Background for the Image of God as Wisdom*

Now we come to the question of why it was the postexilic period, and not some other, that developed a feminine-oriented image of God. I will treat the question here briefly, as the scope of this essay requires, and therefore I will not be able to give an exhaustive answer.

As Rainer Albertz, Frank Crüsemann, and others have impressively shown in a variety of short essays in recent years,[18] the so-called "crisis of wisdom" in Israel was not an intellectual development but a social crisis with complex political, economic, and social bases that were then reflected on and assimilated intellectually in terms of "wisdom." Applied to our concrete question, this means that the Wisdom image of God in the postexilic period should also be understood as a reaction to the special situation of that epoch. It seems to me that Claudia Camp has rightly perceived an important cause of the much-cited remoteness of the God of Israel in the exilic and postexilic period, namely that the kingship, which had been a religious and sacral mediating agency between YHWH and Israel, had disappeared.[19] Now in place of the kingship, as in the pre-monarchical period, the tribe, the family, and the household community resumed their roles as places of revelation. In the postexilic period the household was not only the primary socio-economic unit, but also the determiner of the character and identity of Israelite social existence in this as in all non-monarchical periods.

After the collapse of the monarchy the integrity of the family preserved Israel's covenant relationship with God, and the essential basis for the high regard of women in Wisdom as well as the alteration of the image of God connected with it may well lie in the changed socio-religious context of the era. The book of Proverbs closes with praise of the capable woman, who appears to be the source and center of the identity of the whole household. The house is hers, and *šalōm* issues from her work and her fear of God. Personified Wisdom also appears as one who builds a house, a co-creator, for after the exile women were equally involved in the rebuilding. According to Neh 5:1-5 they felt as responsible for house and property as their husbands. Hence it is probably no accident that as early as Deutero- and Trito-Isaiah (Isaiah 40–66) the mother and family have regained their religious significance and the image of God is more maternal.[20]

The female image of Wisdom the counselor thus has its origin in the household and family, and it achieved significance in an era when there were no longer any kings in Israel, and therefore no court advisors. *Ḥokmā* herself takes the place of the king endowed with wisdom. She is a universal counselor, not the advisor of the king of Israel, but of all kings and even of the already legendary King Solomon. According to Claudia Camp the significance of Wisdom's counter-image, namely folly, can also be deciphered when placed against the historical background sketched here.[21] The fact that there were women who counseled both good and bad may be reason enough for the division into a double image of Wisdom and Folly. However, that does not explain why the seductions of Lady Folly are for the most part rendered concrete in terms of adultery, and why she herself appears in the image of the strange woman and a despised worshiper of goddesses. Probably the motives for this development are intimately connected with Israel's distancing of itself from other religious cults and with the prohibition on marriages with foreign women under Nehemiah, which was meant to serve the cause of stabilization of the internal order in Jerusalem and Judah. According to Mal 2:14-16; 3:5 cases of adultery and divorce multiplied in the Persian period, and according to Neh 13:23-27 the practice of intermarriage with foreign women from Ashdod, Ammon, and Moab had increased as well. Lady Folly, who seduces men to adultery, the strange (or "foreign") woman and follower of foreign cults, may be the symbol of the danger of loss of social and religious identity at a time when marriage and family were all that could guarantee that identity for Israel.

6. Wisdom as Counselor:
Source for a Feminist Christian Spirituality Today?

In concluding, I want to return to the questions posed at the outset. Does the role of Sophia as counselor, which I have been investigating here, offer something persuasive for a feminist Christian theology and spirituality?

Feminist spirituality always seeks to start from life, that is, from human and especially from women's experience.[22] Christian women throughout the world find themselves in the roles of advisors and counselors, especially in the realms of Church and politics. In the wise women of Israel and in *Hokmā* they can find empowering and encouraging prototypes who enunciate the present concerns of women to an astonishing degree. The wise counselors and counseling Wisdom herself, after all, intervene with their counsel and decisions on behalf of justice, but especially for life, the life of the people, the survival of a city or an individual, the lives of the widows and the suffering, life in the future. And it is also the experience of women then and now that this counsel is often thrown to the winds by those in power: "but those who miss me injure themselves; all who hate me love death," says Wisdom in Prov 8:36. This initiative against necrophilia and for life should be more current and relevant today than ever in the face of global threats brought on by patriarchy.

Hokmā the counselor is embedded in a very complex female image of God. She is a creative figure, a woman filled with self-awareness who is not afraid to praise herself. She can be wrathful, and she comes forth promising to proclaim her teaching. All these characteristics correspond very little or not at all to the ruling androcentric image of women—which in itself constitutes a challenge to a feminist confrontation with this different female image. In addition, through reflective mythology Wisdom integrates a multitude of images, symbols, and characteristics of the Ancient Near Eastern goddesses.

The Wisdom image of God in the early Jewish period, as Felix Christ, Max Küchler, Elisabeth Schüssler Fiorenza, and others have so impressively shown,[23] shaped youthful Christianity and its writings to an extent that can scarcely be overestimated. Jesus and John regard themselves as emissaries of Sophia, and Sophia christology may well be one of the Church's oldest, recognizing in Jesus himself the figure of Wisdom, the one sent by God, rejected by human beings, and so returned once again to heaven. We can rightly revive this buried tradition as both Jewish and Christian.

In all this, Sophia meets a great need of Christian women for new images, and at the same time she stands within an ancient biblical tradition.[24] She integrates the goddess without abandoning Judeo-Christian monotheism. She is a mediatrix between God and humanity, heaven and earth, like Jesus Christ, and thus, through her, transcendence and heaven are combined with the female. Biblical Sophia meets the desires of feminist theology to integrate human experience rather than dividing and demonizing it, to seek union and community rather than separation and difference. She builds bridges because she is interactive and open; she includes instead of excluding. In a world where divisions (splitting of atoms, dualism, apartheid, sexism, antisemitism, north-south conflicts) concretely threaten our lives daily this integrative, unifying function of a Christian Sophia spirituality appears to be a promising way into the future, into a world of justice, peace, and respect for creation. Such experiences are grand signs of hope. We may hope, in conclusion, that the wise counsels of Christian women will not be tossed to the wind by the responsible (male) authorities in the Church, but will be listened to in time, because it is also true of them that

> Happy are they who listen to Wisdom,
>   watching daily at her gates,
>   waiting beside her doors.
> For whoever finds Wisdom finds life
>   and obtains favor from YHWH (Prov 8:34-35*).

NOTES

1. Marie-Theres Wacker, "Gefährliche Erinnerungen. Feministische Blicke auf die hebräische Bibel," in eadem, ed., *Theologie feministisch* (Düsseldorf: Patmos, 1988) 14–58. Cf. also eadem, "Die Göttin kehrt zurück. Kritische Sichtung neuerer Entwürfe," in eadem, ed., *Der Gott der Männer und die Frauen* (Düsseldorf: Patmos, 1987) 11–37.

2. At this point let me mention especially the scholarly works of Susan Cady, Marian Ronan, and Hal Taussig, *Sophia. The Future of Feminist Spirituality* (San Francisco: Harper & Row, 1986) and Elisabeth Schüssler Fiorenza, *In Memory of Her. A Feminist Theological Reconstruction of Christian Origins* (New York: Crossroad, 1983). Cf. also Bernhard Lang, *Wisdom and the Book of Proverbs. A Hebrew Goddess Redefined* (New York: Pilgrim, 1986); Urs Winter, *Frau und Göttin.* OBO 53 (Fribourg: Universitätsverlag; Göttingen: Vandenhoeck & Ruprecht, 1983) 508–29; Silvia Schroer, "Die Zweiggöttin in Palästina/Israel. Von der Mittelbronze IIB-Zeit bis zu Jesus Sirach," in Max Küchler and

Christoph Uehlinger, eds., *Jerusalem. Texte, Bilder, Steine.* NTOAG (Fribourg: Universitätsverlag; Göttingen: Vandenhoeck & Ruprecht, 1987) 201–25.

3. Lang, *Wisdom and the Book of Proverbs*, especially at 60–70; cf. also Winter, *Frau und Göttin* 514ff.

4. This author investigates the connection of personified Wisdom and the image of women in the book of Proverbs to the older Israelite traditions, using a literary-critical approach. For what follows see especially Claudia Camp, *Wisdom and the Feminine in the Book of Proverbs* (Decatur, Ga.: Almond Press, 1985) 79–147, 255–82.

5. Athalya Brenner, *The Israelite Woman: Social Role and Literary Type in Biblical Narrative* (Sheffield: JSOT Press, 1985), especially at 33–45, has gone more thoroughly into the question of the various meanings of "being wise" and "wisdom" in connection with women.

6. Cf. Camp, *Wisdom and the Feminine* 120–21.

7. See below, Chapter 5.

8. On this see in detail Elisabeth Schüssler Fiorenza, *In Memory of Her* 115–18.

9. Camp, *Wisdom and the Feminine* 86–90. The author rejects, on good grounds, any hasty distinction between good and bad advice or counsel and between encouragement to action and seduction.

10. See, however, the translation by Dieter Georgi, *Weisheit Salomos.* Jüdische Schriften aus hellenistisch-römischer Zeit 3/4 (Gütersloh: Gerd Mohn, 1980), especially of Wis 7:28–8:18. Georgi's translation is faithful to the erotic coloring of the original.

11. On the general context see Max Küchler, *Schweigen, Schmuck und Schleier. Drei neutestamentliche Vorschriften zur Verdrängung der Frauen auf dem Hintergrund einer frauenfeindlichen Exegese des Alten Testaments im antiken Judentum.* NTOA 1 (Fribourg: Universitätsverlag; Göttingen: Vandenhoeck & Ruprecht, 1986).

12. Georg Molin, "Die Stellung der Gebira im Staate Juda," *ThZ* 10 (1954) 161–75; Herbert Donner, "Art und Herkunft des Amtes der Königinmutter im Alten Testament," in Richard von Kienle, et al., eds., *Festschrift Johannes Friedrich zum 65. Geburtstag am 27. August 1958 gewidmet* (Heidelberg: C. Winter, 1959) 105–45; Gösta W. Ahlström, *Aspects of Syncretism in Israelite Religion.* Horae Soederblomianae V (Lund: Gleerup, 1963) 57–88. These older contributions are in need of a feminist revision.

13. Niels-Erik A. Andreasen, "The Role of the Queen Mother in Israelite Society," *CBQ* 45 (1983) 179–94; Ihromi, "Die Königinmutter und der ʿamm haʾarez im Reich Juda," *VT* 24 (1974) 421–29; Sonia Acker-

mann, "The Queen Mother and the Cult in Israel," *JBL* 112 (1993) 385–401; Renate Jost, *Frauen, Männer und die Himmelskönigin.* Exegetische Studien (Gütersloh: Gerd Mohn, 1995) 141–46.

14. Cf. Wacker, "Gefährliche Erinnerungen," and for the cult of Asherah see Silvia Schroer, *In Israel gab es Bilder.* OBO 74 (Fribourg: Universitätsverlag; Göttingen: Vandenhoeck & Ruprecht, 1987) 21–45.

15. Cf. Camp, *Wisdom and the Feminine* 199–200; 278–79.

16. Pieter A. H. deBoer, "The Counsellor," in Martin Noth and D. Winton Thomas, eds., *Wisdom in Israel and in the Ancient Near East. Presented to Professor Harold Henry Rowley by the Society for Old Testament Study in Association with the Editorial Board of Vetus Testamentum in Celebration of his Sixty-Fifth Birthday, 24 March 1955.* VT.S 3 (Leiden: Brill, 1955) 42–71.

17. Ibid. 59. DeBoer's suggestion has apparently not been heeded (cf., e.g., Winter, *Frau und Göttin* 644–48).

18. Rainer Albertz, "Der sozialgeschichtliche Hintergrund des Hiobbuches und der 'Babylonischen Theodizee,'" in Jörg Jeremias and Lothar Perlitt, eds., *Die Botschaft und die Boten. Festschrift für Hans Walter Wolff zum 70. Geburtstag* (Neukirchen-Vluyn: Neukirchener Verlag, 1981) 349–72; Frank Crüsemann, "Die unveränderbare Welt. Überlegungen zur 'Krisis der Weisheit' beim Prediger (Kohelet)," in Willy Schottroff and Wolfgang Stegemann, eds., *Der Gott der kleinen Leute. Sozialgeschichtliche Bibelauslegungen 1: Altes Testament* (Munich: Kaiser, 1979) 80–104. (English: "The Unchangeable World: The 'Crisis of Wisdom' in Koheleth," in *God of the Lowly: Socio-historical Interpretations of the Bible.* Translated by Matthew J. O'Connell [Maryknoll, N.Y.: Orbis, 1984] 57–77.) Cf. also Silvia Schroer, "Entstehungsgeschichtliche und gegenwärtige Situierungen des Hiob-Buches," in Ökumenischer Arbeitskreis für Bibelarbeit, ed., *Hiob* (Basel and Einsiedeln, 1989).

19. At this point I can only refer to the foundational book by Claudia Camp (*Wisdom and the Feminine* 227–91) and cite the conclusions of her work in a few theses.

20. Although by a different route, Erhard S. Gerstenberger arrives at very similar conclusions in his little book, *Jahwe, ein patriarchaler Gott? Traditionelles Gottesbild und Feministische Theologie* (Stuttgart: Kohlhammer, 1988), especially at 17–27. The book is well worth reading. See the English translation: *Yahweh—The Patriarch: Ancient Images of God and Feminist Theology.* Translated by Frederick J. Gaiser (Minneapolis: Fortress, 1996).

21. Cf. Camp, *Wisdom and the Feminine* 112–19; 265–71.

22. Cf. Cady, Ronan, and Taussig, *Sophia,* especially 1–15. I see the considerations that follow as suggestions. They cannot be and are not intended to be answers to the many unresolved historical questions about *Ḥokmā.*

23. Felix Christ, *Jesus Sophia. Die Sophia-Christologie bei den Synoptikern.* AThANT 57 (Zürich: Zwingli-Verlag, 1970); Max Küchler, *Frühjüdische Weisheitstraditionen. Zum Fortgang weisheitlichen Denkens im Bereich des frühjüdischen Jahwe-Glaubens.* OBO 26 (Fribourg: Universitätsverlag; Göttingen: Vandenhoeck & Ruprecht, 1979) 584–86; Elisabeth Schüssler Fiorenza, *In Memory of Her.* See also my essay mentioned in n. 2 above as well as Chapter 9 of the present book.

24. For what follows see Cady, Ronan, and Taussig, *Sophia,* especially 76–93.

CHAPTER FOUR

"And When the Next War Began . . . ."
The Wise Woman of Abel of Beth-maacah
(2 Samuel 20:14-22)

The short narrative about the wise woman in Abel of Beth-maacah is one of the little-known stories in the First Testament. When I write about this wise woman today, in a time where new wars are continually breaking out all over the world, I do so with great sorrow and desperation. The voices of those who desire peace are not listened to. The opportunities to prevent senseless wars are repeatedly squandered. I can only read the text against this background, and encourage women to enter into the inheritance of the woman of Abel of Beth-maacah. Her message is a word of reason: war is not a political tool. This message is addressed to the responsible men who are continually preparing for war, planning it, carrying it out—and to the many who are silent.

1. Rescue from Danger

This story is part of a narrative cycle about the struggle and confusion surrounding the choice of a successor for David, the first king of Judah and Israel (2 Samuel 9–20; 1 Kings 1–2). David has to assert his authority over his own sons, who begin quarreling over the throne while he is still alive. Now, in addition, Sheba son of Bichri, a Benjaminite, raises a rebellion against him. Sheba gathers mercenaries and troops from the northern kingdom of Israel to fight for political autonomy (2 Sam 20:1). This uprising is a serious threat to David, because his empire is in danger of falling apart. So David has his general, Joab, pursue Sheba. Sheba flees to the city of Abel of Beth-maacah and digs in there (2 Sam 20:14). Swiftly, Joab and his men begin to erect siege works in order to draw the whole city into the fight.

In this dangerous situation into which the otherwise neutral inhabitants of Abel of Beth-maacah have fallen, a wise woman ascends the broad defensive wall of the city and, in the hearing and sight of all those in the city and outside the walls, demands to speak with Joab, the field commander, in person. He does, in fact, enter into dialogue with her. The nameless woman speaks with Joab, who is standing below her perch on the wall. She does not waste words, but asks a few brief questions. Abel, she says, was always a city (like Dan) where people could seek counsel. Abel was a "mother in Israel," that is, a place where advice and counsel were given by (professional or volunteer) sages. And now is that no longer true? Abel, a city of YHWH, is to be destroyed? Joab is in a bind. No, of course he does not want to destroy the entire city. He asks for the head of the traitor Sheba and promises that he will then withdraw. The wise woman agrees, without waiting for a decision from her fellow citizens, who are probably terrified. Only afterward does she go to the people "with her wise plan," and her decision is accepted. Sheba's head is thrown over the wall, and the bloody slaughter is averted.

2. The Wise Women of Israel

We can only grasp the full significance of the "wise woman" of Abel of Beth-maacah if we view her alongside other wise women in the First Testament. "To be wise" in Israel did not mean simply being "smart" or "educated," but above all being "experienced." Thus there is an enormous history and literary tradition of women, wives, and mothers in Israel who were counselors, who handed on their life experience in a variety of ways.

Besides the woman of Abel of Beth-maacah, we know of a "wise woman" from Tekoa whom this same Joab summons in 2 Samuel 14 to aid him in the carrying out of his plan. She is to cunningly persuade King David not to continue the banishment of his

son Absalom. The women of Tekoa and Abel of Beth-maacah
seem to have held an office called "wise woman." They appeal to
Wisdom traditions, are masters of the art of diplomacy, and employ all their skill on behalf of the life of an individual or a whole
community. Their influence was great and their counsel was
highly prized, so much so that they were even summoned before
kings.

In a broader sense Abigail, one of David's wives (1 Samuel 25),
also belongs among the "wise women," as does the widow Judith,
through whose advice and action the city of Bethulia and the
whole of Israel were saved from being destroyed by the Assyrians.

Besides these "wise women," who were "official" advisors and
exercised their offices in the public forum, the First Testament is
aware of a great number of wives who advised their husbands.
Thus, for example, the childless Sarah counsels her husband Abraham to beget an heir with the slave woman, Hagar (Gen 16:2).
Thanks to the advice and aid of his wife Michal, David is able to
flee from his enemy, King Saul (1 Sam 19:11). Next to household
duties, the advisory function may well have been the most important role of an Israelite woman. Although the numerous texts
about wives who give advice are very realistic in presenting both
good and bad advisors it is noteworthy that there is scarcely a case
in which the husband does not listen to his wife. The (good) wife
was valued in Israel as a representative of Wisdom; it is said of
wives as of *Hokmā* (Wisdom) that they are of more value than
jewels and that they come from YHWH (Prov 3:15; 31:10; 19:14;
Sir 1:1), that is, they are a gift of God.

A third type of wise woman is the mother who gives counsel.
Like fathers, mothers also give advice to their children in the book
of Proverbs. In the southern kingdom of Judah the mother of the
reigning king achieved a very influential status; she was the "mistress of the royal household" who gave the king political advice.
Her authority must have been considerable (think of Bathsheba,
for example: cf. 1 Kings 2:13-23). That explains why in Judg 5:7
Deborah is called a "mother" in Israel. She is a counselor of signal
importance for Israel's future; like a prophet she proclaims God's
will. Thus a city like Abel of Beth-maacah can be called a "mother
in Israel," a place of counsel. Against this background it is even

more obvious that the wise woman of Abel of Beth-maacah is a figure who makes divine Wisdom and the divine will visible.

In the postexilic period there arose in the milieu of the teachers of Wisdom the image of personified Wisdom, *Hokmā*. In the late writings of the First Testament *Hokmā* occupies a considerable amount of space: she appears in Proverbs 1–9, Job 28, some chapters of Sirach, and finally in the Wisdom of Solomon (Wisdom 6–9). The figure of divine Wisdom subsumes the roles of the various counseling women of Israel. Only on the basis of the experience of and with these wise women could Wisdom appear as a counselor (Prov 8:12-16; Wis 8:9). In the postexilic period it is *Hokmā* herself who stands teaching and preaching before the city gates, addressing the men and all the people of Israel (Prov 1:20-33; 8:1-36).

3. Then a head rolled . . .

But what message does the woman in the narrative in 2 Samuel 20 have for us today? Is this not just another bloody story, typical of the First Testament, which in general is not exactly prudish about stories of murder, mass killing, and all kinds of violence? To put it more bluntly: can a woman who has someone's head cut off and thrown over the wall be a model for us?

It may be worthwhile to work our way into the story and the woman herself, to feel what she feels. Certainly a man is killed in this story. But he is a military leader, not an asylum-seeker. Sheba has drawn a neutral city into a deadly conflict.

In the end *one* man is killed. How many human lives would a battle for the city have cost? How much misery would have fallen on innocent women, children, and old people? The wise woman's decision was the only rational one in this crisis situation. Even so, she would certainly have preferred to avoid *any* bloodshed. The woman of Abel of Beth-maacah is a woman of peace. She accepts her heavy responsibility; she exposes herself by appearing in public, standing unhesitatingly on the wall. She demands that those responsible listen to her. Her speech is clear, brief, and to the point. She claims God's support in her words and in her actions. The city and its inhabitants are the heritage of YHWH (v. 19).

4. A Fantasy of the Distant Future?

War and destruction are senseless: that is the message of the woman of Abel of Beth-maacah. It is a rational message. And it is no accident that this message is delivered by a woman.

The story in the book of Samuel always reminds me of the poem "Fantasy of the Distant Future" by Erich Kästner. There it is also women who see to it that the war the men want to provoke cannot break out. They lock their men in the house, turn the responsible leaders over their knees and announce that there will be no war.

Certainly a military operation that brings suffering and misery to helpless populations can no longer be prevented by the courageous protest of a single wise woman. But if many women today had, or would take steps to learn the self-confidence of the wise women of Israel, we could better and more conclusively resist, together, the manifold death-dealing machinery of patriarchy. From the woman of Abel of Beth-maacah we learn what it means to take the initiative for peace, to make difficult decisions alone, but with courage. For peace has its price: if we resist discord and war we will always get our hands dirty, make mistakes, even come to wrong decisions. But we will break our silence; we will practice speaking publicly, demanding that people (men) listen to us. And we will speak and act in the name of God before the men in power. For God is a God who puts an end to wars; God's power does not rest on strong men and big armies, for God is a God of the small and the weak.

I think we cannot do without the woman of Abel of Beth-maacah and the many other great women of the Bible. We need these mothers and sisters of our faith in our struggle for a more just world without patriarchal organization and without wars.

Fantasy of the Distant Future

And when the next war began,
the women said "No!"
and locked their brothers, sons, and husbands
securely in the house.

Then in every country, it seems,
they went to the head man's place

with thick canes in their hands
and hauled the guys outside.

They laid those guys across their knees,
the ones who ordered the war:
the bankers and industrialists,
the ministers and the generals.

More than one cane was broken in two,
and many a big mouth was silenced.
There was a lot of shouting in every land,
but nowhere was there war.

The women went home again,
to their brothers and sons and husbands,
and told them the war was canceled!
The men stared out of the windows
and wouldn't look at the women . . .[1]

5. Suggestions for Practical Bible Study

Preliminary Remarks

This story has the advantage of being almost unknown, very
short, and presenting a simple set of actions. Scarcely any additional information is needed for people to understand it. What is
problematic is that European and North American women at first
react with aversion to "violence." That reaction can cause them to
block out things and makes access to the text difficult. It is very
important to give enough time to this first emotional reaction to
the story in Phase I. When the participants have expressed their
shock or resistance they have already overcome the first barrier.
The fundamental problem of the use of violent force is not solved
by the story, but it does demand that we make some distinctions in
our judgments regarding violence. Variant III B (Phase III) may
require the assistance of a woman who is experienced in matters
of body language, movement, dance, rhythm training, and the like.

I. Approaching the Biblical Text

Preparation: Place chairs in a circle. In the center, place a symbol of
the wise woman of Abel of Beth-maacah: a stone or a cloth.

Step One: Read the story out loud.

Step Two: A conversation with the woman. We introduce ourselves to the woman, who is seated in the middle. What would we like to say? What questions would we like to ask her?

II. Listening to the Biblical Text

Preparation: Provide pencils and markers, large and small pieces of paper, and a copy of the biblical text for each woman.

Step One: In small groups of five or six, the participants should do the following:

- Divide the text into scenes. It can be separated into five scenes according to place and actors:

    Scene 1 (v. 14): Sheba on his victorious march through Israel to Abel of Beth-maacah.

    Scene 2 (v. 15): Joab lays siege to Abel of Beth-maacah.

    Scene 3 (vv. 16-21): The conversation between the wise woman on the city wall and Joab.

    Scene 4 (v. 22a): The wise woman persuades her fellow citizens that their safety will cost Sheba's head.

    Scene 5 (v. 22b): Sheba's head is thrown to Joab.

    Scene 6 (v. 22c): Joab withdraws.

- Draw the principal scenes in the story on large sheets (sketches only). Or: compose headlines for each scene, to be hung on a kiosk.

- Consider how the woman acted. What steps did she take? Write them down in detail!

Step Two: The small groups present their results to the whole group; all together discuss the following questions:

- What arguments does the woman use in her conversation with Joab?

- What do you think is the basis of the woman's wisdom?

- To what authority does she appeal?

III. Taking the Biblical Text Farther

A biblical story can only be an impulse to liberation for us as women today if we *carefully* apply it to our own situation.

Possibility A

Preparation: Each woman is given a copy of Erich Kästner's poem.

Step One: Someone reads the Kästner poem out loud.

Step Two: The following questions should provoke discussion of the problem of women and war:

• To what extent is the situation of that woman at all comparable to our situation? (Men make war; women fight for life.)

• To what extent is the story not at all comparable to our reality?

Step Three: It is time to consider how the "wise woman" can encourage me/us. For every step she takes in the story,

1. getting up on the "city wall,"

2. calling on those responsible to dialogue with her,

3. demanding attention,

4. speaking clearly,

5. making decisions alone,

look for corresponding instances of women's wisdom today and use them to compose an appeal to women, ten commandments for women, or slogans for a women's demonstration.

Possibility B: Body-language

Step One: Each woman in turn stands alone at one end of a large room. The other women sit next to each other on the floor at the other end. The one woman walks across the room toward the others, without speaking. She walks deliberately, imagining that, like the woman of Abel of Beth-maacah, she has something important to say to them, there below the wall. She stands before them and attempts to make eye contact with all the other women. Nothing is said. Instead of words, the woman attempts to use a gesture, a movement that expresses her desires, her feelings. Then she seats herself and the process is repeated until all the women have had a turn.

Step Two: Discussion. How did I experience *myself,* and how did I experience *the others?* (posture, walk, feelings that arose, eye contact, etc.). It is good to have a woman with some experience in such exercises present.

What did we learn from this "game" about ourselves and the wise woman?

NOTE

1. From Erich Kästner, *Gedichte* (Frankfurt: 1981) 157. For recent literature on the material in this chapter, see Silvia Schroer, *Die Samuelbücher.* NSK.AT 7 (Stuttgart: Kohlhammer, 1992).

CHAPTER FIVE

Abigail: A Wise Woman Works for Peace

The long story of Abigail in 1 Samuel 25 is one of the less-well-known stories of women in the First Testament. She does not appear in most of the newer collections or periodical special issues on biblical women—an injustice, it seems to me.

Abigail was the wife of a wealthy man, the owner of large flocks and herds; his name was Nabal and he came from Maon in southern Judah. He was known in the neighborhood not only for his wealth, but also because of his stupidity, coupled with obstinacy (Nabal means "fool") and coarseness. His wife, in contrast, was famous for her cleverness and beauty, and in the course of the narrative it becomes clear that she is very articulate and is accustomed to acting independently and courageously.

At the time of the sheep-shearing festival in Carmel, David, who is hiding from Saul with his guerrilla band in the wilderness of Paran, sends ten men to Nabal. They are to ask Nabal to reward them for the fact that David and his band have done no harm to Nabal's shepherds while they were pasturing their sheep; on the contrary, they had protected them from other bands. Nabal, in his greed, is completely blind to the way things are; he sends these "men who come from I do not know where" back to David empty-handed. David, enraged, gives the command to his men to strap on their swords and start out for Carmel to take bloody revenge for this insult to his honor and the injustice done him.

In the meantime Abigail has learned from a servant what has taken place, and she acts like lightning to rectify the situation. She has the donkeys loaded with food and rides to meet David, without saying a word to her husband. David, muttering angrily to himself, is already on the way to Carmel with four hundred men. When Abigail comes face to face with this troop she gets down from her donkey and throws herself on the ground before David. Before he can say a word she begins a long speech that we can well regard as a rhetorical masterpiece. In the first place, she emphasizes her submissiveness by repeatedly addressing David as "my lord" and calling herself "your servant." Moreover, she skillfully attempts to bring David to accept her gifts, both by means of arguments and through flattery and appeasement; she seems to be embarrassed neither by the flattery nor by the arguments. First she tells David that Nabal, because of his stupidity, was in any case not the right person to deal with David's emissaries, and that she herself had unfortunately not seen them. She thus pretends to take the blame on herself while really excusing the whole affair by declaring her husband irresponsible. Abigail's second argument shows her to be a devoted adherent of YHWH. David is not unnecessarily to soil his hands with blood, because God has greater things in mind for him. David will found a house, a dynasty. These far-seeing prophecies are accompanied by powerful blessings implored for David and equally powerful curses against all his enemies.

David's response to this skillfully crafted torrent of words confirms that Abigail has calculated correctly. In particular the second argument, and of course the accompanying gifts, do in fact bring David to his senses and cause his wrath to dissipate. Abigail rides home and finds that her husband has gotten very drunk at the sheep-shearing festival; hence it is only on the following morning that she can report to him what she has done. The news hits Nabal like a stroke—literally—and ten days later he dies, with some additional divine assistance. David hears of this immediately and with great satisfaction, and sends messengers without delay to "woo" Abigail and make her his wife. She seems to have been expecting exactly that; again affirming her ready willingness to serve, she goes with the messengers unhesitatingly.

We hear very little of Abigail afterward. She accompanies David into exile among the Philistines, is kidnapped from Ziklag by the Amalekites, brought back by David, and gives birth to a son in

Hebron. However, neither she nor her son play any role in Jerusalem. The story of the beautiful and clever Abigail is especially interesting to me because from a feminist perspective, somewhat like the book of Ruth, it cannot be pressed flat in one or another direction. The story has a will of its own, so to speak, and I let it have its way by looking at its contradictions without resolving them, by pursuing in all its differentiated ways the manner in which Abigail fits herself into the vast field of tension between patriarchal oppression and women's liberation.

Thus the principal actor in the whole narrative is Abigail, but when we look at the context it is clear that the story fits within the corpus of David-traditions and tells anecdotally how David obtained this wife from Carmel. The extent to which the details are historical is not very important; the image of a woman in a fictional story can also have historical and sociological value. What is historically important is that David was able, through a clever marital politics, to establish good relationships with the respectable families in the piedmont regions in the south of Judea by taking Abigail and Ahinoam of Jezreel (1 Sam 25:43) as his wives.

Abigail is thus not an ordinary woman of Judea. She comes from a wealthy house and is worthy to be the wife of the future king of Israel. Hence it is no surprise that the narrator is interested in displaying all the special qualities and virtues of this woman, above all her cleverness and, of course, her beauty. He succeeds in this by contrasting Abigail from the outset with a negative figure, her husband Nabal, who is not only foolish but also stubborn and mean, in short, a monster and a tyrant. I know of scarcely any other story in the First Testament in which the cleverness of a woman is so consistently given a positive evaluation, or in which a man is branded thus *a priori* with such a negative cliché.

Abigail's cleverness is demonstrated in a number of ways in the narrative. She recognizes immediately and with a great deal of foresight what will be the consequences of her husband's stubborn attitude; she acts independently, quickly, and with determination; and she knows how to talk.

Abigail is a woman who acts for peace. She attempts to prevent war between men that will bring misery to her whole household, a men's war brought on by stupidity, stubbornness, wounded male honor, and wrath. She makes common cause with the little people, her shepherds, who already sense what has happened. Abigail's concern is for life, her own and that of her people. Therefore she lets everything ride on one card: she compromises her husband and repudiates him completely; she risks handing herself over, a woman alone, to David and his men; she takes all the blame on herself and submits herself to David in gesture and in word.

When life is at stake, either physical existence or life in freedom, all means are fair: but are these not, after all, typical feminine wiles—tricks and concealment (as regards Nabal), (false) admission of guilt and submission to the more powerful? Other women in the First Testament (Lot's daughters, Tamar, Jael, Ruth, Judith) are also quick to employ these feminine tricks in accomplishing their heroic deeds, in order to reach their goal.

Much less typical in this sense is the way Abigail presents herself as the emissary of YHWH sent to preserve David from serious blood-guilt: "Now then, my lord, as the LORD lives, and as you yourself live, since the LORD has restrained you from bloodguilt and from taking vengeance with your own hand . . ." (25:26). This is clearly the theological center of the narrative. This woman, Abigail, speaks in the name of YHWH when she attempts to deter David from carrying out his bloody plans. God sends this woman to David to make the divine will known to him, and Abigail is in this moment God's prophet. In fact, David confirms it: "Blessed be the LORD, the God of Israel, who sent you to meet me today! Blessed be your good sense, and blessed be you, who have kept me today from bloodguilt and from avenging myself by my own hand!" (25:32-33). God is opposed to senseless bloodshed, and it is remarkable in every way that here a woman proclaims this message in the tradition of the great prophets of Israel, and carries God's cause forward successfully.

Abigail's decisive action has another side, however, and we should not lose sight of it. The female figures in the First Testament, much like the depictions of goddesses in Ancient Near Eastern and Israelite art, can be assigned certain roles. Thus there are the "patronesses" or "protectors" (Sarah, Tamar, Rahab, etc.), the "warriors" (Deborah, Jael, Judith), the "mediators" (Esther, etc.). Abigail is one of the mediators. She mediates between two parties in conflict, and she also mediates between God and humanity. Here we can again ask: is this not a typical role for women in patriarchy—when women, their whole lives long, bear the brunt of the task of preventing the worst conflicts set in motion by men by intervening with their concern, their understanding, their diplomacy, and so on? Can we do anything with a female figure whose principal task (from the narrator's perspective) is to preserve the future king of Israel from having too many stains on his white waistcoat?

For these very reasons it gives me particular satisfaction that in this narrative the profit from Abigail's negotiations does not fall entirely to the men. The woman receives a reward as well in that God personally intervenes and neatly gets rid of the nasty Nabal. What woman, starving for life, would not prefer a young, attractive guerrilla leader to a rich fool and a drunkard? Never mind what Abigail gained from the exchange in the long run. Her traces vanish, like those of so many women, in the sands of male historical writing.

The story of Abigail contributes something to a more subtle reconstruction of women's lives in Israel before and in the early stages of its nationhood. It shows that emancipation even then was related to money, way of life, milieu, and education; that in any case there were women living at the edge of the wilderness who because of their way of life were accustomed to act for themselves and to get along without their husbands (cf. the wise woman of Tekoa in 2 Sam 14:1-21). It shows that in early YHWH-religion the idea that God would make spokespersons of women was not at all offensive, and that women were in command of religious language.

In addition, Abigail seems to have a very thought-provoking biblical message to offer to us middle-class women in Europe or in the United States. While Deborah, Jael, or Judith employed (military) force to resolve conflicts and *therefore* have always been favorite female biblical figures in the history of exegesis (and perhaps even in recent feminist exegesis), the story of Abigail presents an unmistakable plea for diplomacy, negotiation, and non-violence in solving life-threatening conflicts. Making peace demands cleverness, insight, and a readiness to risk something.

Peace cannot be achieved without risk and entirely without sacrifice. Certainly it is easy, after the fact, to accuse people of cowardice, foolishness, or weakness when they have succeeded, through peaceful means, in preventing the escalation of violence. But negotiations, compromises, and sometimes even giving in undoubtedly require more intelligence and courage than the mobilization of any kind of military force.

I cannot speak for the women in South Africa or Central America or even for women who are constantly subjected to male violence in their private lives. I do not know what Abigail could say to them. But for all the women among us who are in the "peace movement" Abigail could be a sister and a companion in the struggle. When men go over our heads to prepare for war and drive the earth closer and closer to ecological bankruptcy we are summoned, like Abigail—without asking our husbands or any man—to take steps for peace; we are called to independent and courageous action. When, over our heads, the interests of the wealthy industrial nations are "defended" at the expense of our sisters and brothers in the so-called Third World we are obligated—without waiting for assent or recognition from any authority—to make common cause with the little people there; then we are called as Christians—without waiting for our churches—to sharpen our tongues and to speak in the name of God on behalf of peace. For it is God who is the advocate of the "clever women for peace," and God will bring their cause to fulfillment.[1]

NOTE

1. For further literature on this topic see Silvia Schroer, *Die Samuelbücher.* NSK.AT (Stuttgart: 1992).

CHAPTER SIX

The One Lord and Male Dominance in the Book of Jesus Sirach: The Image of Woman and the Image of Wisdom in a Misogynist Document

It would be negligent to leave aside the book of Sirach when one is undertaking a feminist investigation of the texts in which personified Wisdom plays a role. The misogyny of this book, written around the beginning of the second century B.C.E. and—a unique instance among First Testament books—traceable to a single male author, is proverbial. A significant portion of the teaching of Jesus ben Sira, which according to the introduction to the book was translated from Hebrew into Greek by his grandson in Egypt some time after 117 B.C.E. (only the Greek text has survived in full),[1] is devoted to the topic of "women" (Sir 3:2-16; 7:19-27; 9:1-9; 22:4-5; 23:16-27; 25:13–26:27; 36:23-27; 41:20-22; 42:6-14; 47:19-20, and elsewhere). But personified *Ḥokmā* also plays an important part in the collection of Ben Sira's teachings. The opening chapter (1:1-30), ch. 24, and the connecting section between the two main parts of the book, as well as a hymn at the very end (51:13-30) are devoted to her; these parts are given significant weight and extensive treatment. Add to this the poems on Wisdom in 4:11-19; 6:18-37; 14:20–15:8.[2] One is almost forced, therefore, to take a closer look at the connection between the author's image of women and the figure of Wisdom. The notion that there is such a connection is suggested by the investigation of other Wisdom books. *Ḥokmā* or Sophia does not exist independently of these writings, and as a personification she fulfills a special function, closely adapted to the content of the individual books. At this point I should emphasize, of course, that there has long been a need for a basic feminist engagement with the whole book, and that cannot be done in this one chapter.[3] Moreover, the dominant exegesis leaves much to be desired as regards social-historical questions, with the result that there are some quite contradictory opinions in circulation regarding the role and purposes of Ben Sira within his Jewish-Hellenistic context.[4] Recent works on the lives of women in Greco-Roman Palestine continue to provide fascinating information on the broader context of the document.[5] They show in impressive fashion how great was the heterogeneity of Second Temple Judaism and also challenge us to a precise hearing of the voice of Jesus Sirach within this mighty chorus.

1. Jesus Sirach's Image of Woman

The first part of the book (chs. 2–23) contains Wisdom teachings for the life of the individual, especially in daily married life and in the family. In the second part (chs. 24–50) the topic is social ethics in the larger community. Chapters 44–50 introduce a new element in Israel's Wisdom literature, namely a retrospective view of Israel's history in the form of a laudatory poem on the (male) ancestors. It begins with Enoch and ends with Nehemiah and Simon the high priest. No women appear in this author's vision of Israel's history. On the other hand, it is very important to him to instruct young men about the right way to relate to women. To anticipate my conclusion, I can say that I do not agree with Warren C. Trenchard[6] that Jesus Sirach was unusually misogynistic. Nor do I believe, as Alexander di Lella tries to make us believe in his apologetic commentary,[7] that the times were simply that way and that Jesus Sirach simply could not have had any other view of women. I think, rather, that this author, with great pastoral zeal, has conjured up an androcentric reality-as-he-wishes-it-were. We must read his texts with a feminist hermeneutics of suspicion, seeing them as projections, that is, in the awareness that reality was different from what Ben Sira describes.[8] Concretely, we may suppose that in the second century B.C.E. Jewish women (probably influenced by Hellenism) assumed a greater degree of freedom in public and private life, and that Jewish men saw this as a danger to the (patriarchal) order of things.

Jesus Sirach writes about mothers, widows, daughters, and wives, about courtesans and whores. All of them appear only in relation to or in the eyes of men, never independently and for themselves. It is by no means the case that a unified negative view of women emerges from these verses. In 3:2-16 the author strongly emphasizes the mother's right to be respected by her sons (and that means she is to be supported as well!). Every wrong action toward one's mother is a sin and an offense to the Creator. When it is a question of divine solidarity and the works of mercy, widows and orphans take first place with Jesus Sirach, and like the other Wisdom writers he regards a good wife as a gift from God (26:3, 14-15).

Daughters are a source of concern for their fathers and one must constantly keep an eye on them until they are married (7:24-25; 22:4-5). The longest section on the subject of daughters is in 42:9-15, where the numerous reasons why a man must look out for his daughter are listed: he must be careful that she is not seduced and does not become pregnant, that she does not remain single and fail to get the right man, that she is not barren, and so on. Jesus Sirach recommends that daughters should be kept at home and watched carefully (vv. 11-14):

11 Keep strict watch over a headstrong daughter,
        or she may make you a laughingstock to your enemies, . . .
    See that there is no lattice in her room,
        no spot that overlooks the approaches to the house.
12 Do not let her parade her beauty before any man,
        or spend her time among married women;
13 for from garments comes the moth,
        and from a woman comes woman's wickedness.
14 Better is the wickedness of a man than a woman who
            does good . . .

The rigorous restriction of the freedom of movement of young, unmarried women by no means corresponds to older Israelite tradition. There are numerous indications in all literary genres that young girls in Israel took part in festivals, often unaccompanied, that they went to the fields, met at the wells, and so on. The prohibition against girls' spending time with married women[9] shows that there were still meeting-places for women outside the father's house, even in the author's time. Through his recommendations he attempts to restrict the possibilities for female alliances and solidarity. However, it is very doubtful that he enjoyed much success, because the only men who could take his advice to heart were those who had large households in which a separate room could be provided for the daughters of the family.

A woman, once married, is strictly taboo for all other men. Here Jesus Sirach takes up traditional Wisdom material. Much as in Proverbs 1–9, the subject in a number of passages is "strange" or "loose" women and the consequences of adultery, as well as rules of conduct for young men (9:8-9; 41:20). The Wisdom teacher also urgently recommends having nothing to do with prostitutes and singing girls, not so much on moral grounds as because men are ensnared by women like that (9:3), may be caught by them (9:4), and may lose their possessions (9:6).[10] The warnings against adultery are much more urgent; as in the introduction to Proverbs it is described as a mortal danger (26:22).

The author pays most attention to the behavior of married women, whom he divides into two basic categories, good and bad. This division is made from a purely androcentric perspective; respect and praise belong only to the woman who adapts herself to patriarchal ideas of feminine virtue. The good wife is wise and charming (7:19), she cares for her husband so that he may grow old in peace, she is silent, beautiful, and restrained even toward her husband (26:1-2). Such a wife is a valuable treasure (7:19); she fulfills what Jesus Sirach regards as the order of things laid down in Gen 2:18-25, that the woman should be to the man "a helper fit for him" (36:29). Of course Ben Sira does not understand this, as does the primeval history in Genesis 2, as relationship and support by an equal being, but in the sense of aid through service, being a "pillar of support." A woman's wisdom does not consist, for example, in her fear of God, but in her respect for her husband (26:26). The reversal of this idea makes it abundantly clear that it is a question of the deification of the man, because a woman who rebels against her husband is called godless. In the numerous sayings about bad and wicked women in 25:13–26:27 we often can only conjecture what the real issue may have been: licentiousness, impudence, love of gossip, and—already a theme in Proverbs (Prov 21:9; 27:15, and elsewhere)—the screaming and abuse of an unsatisfied, contentious woman. From the many allusions we can at least gather that women had some influence and power that men feared. Jesus Sirach pities any man who acquires a so-called "bad" wife, and he advises him to separate from her (25:26). In any case if his wife is unreliable he should, if necessary, use seals to protect himself against losses in his household (7:26; 25:26). The ideal wife, on the other hand, is silent and submissive. She is the field in which the man sows his seed (26:19-21) in order to secure posterity for himself.

The teacher of Wisdom fears nothing more than a wife who wants to "rule" herself (26:25), and the overturning of the patriarchal order that occurs when anyone uses violence against the *paterfamilias:*

> 9:2: Do not give yourself to a woman and let her trample down your strength.

> 33:20-23: To son or wife, to brother or friend,
>   do not give power over yourself, as long as you live . . .
>   While you are still alive and have breath in you,
>   do not let anyone take your place. . . .
>   Excel in all that you do. . . .

One statement in the book that has had the most serious consequences is found in 25:24 (Hebrew 25:23) in the context of warnings against bad and self-assertive wives:

> From a woman sin had its beginning,
>   and because of her we all die.

Here we encounter a very successful interpretation of Genesis 2–3, repeated in later Jewish writings and also in 2 Cor 11:3 and 1 Tim

2:14, according to which Eve, though the second to be created, was the first in sin; her offense has saddled all humanity with the fate of mortality.[11] There is no explanation of just what her sin was. The teacher of Wisdom seems to be referring to an interpretation of Genesis 2–3 that was well known in Jerusalem. The statement breathes a profound contempt for the female sex; it is introduced in this context to consolidate patriarchal claims to power and to elevate them to the religious plane in order thereby to shatter every kind of female resistance to the world of men.

Jesus Sirach's remarks on women may have been influenced in many ways by Egyptian Wisdom teachings, especially those from the fourth and third centuries B.C.E.[12] The Egyptian teachings are also addressed to young men. Although women are not addressed, they are talked about, characterized, and classified, so that the young men may behave appropriately. While in the teachings of Ani from the 18th dynasty (probably stemming from the mid-fourteenth century B.C.E.) men were warned not to be quarrelsome or to treat their wives unjustly (vv. 315-329), the teachings of Ankh-Sheshonki from the fourth century paint images of women that are similar to those of Jesus Sirach, although no Egyptian teaching yields anything to the Jerusalem Wisdom teacher when it comes to misogyny:

> 174-178: Do not open your heart to your wife; what you tell her
>   goes on the street.
>   Tell it to your mother; she is a discreet woman.
>   A woman is (only) interested in what she understands.
>   Teaching a woman is like trying to fill a sack with sand when
>   it has a hole in the side.

The Egyptian sages also esteemed mothers (Teaching of Ani vv. 242-261) and clever wives; there are many sayings that praise them. There are constant warnings against relationships with strange women and against adultery (Ankh-Sheshonki vv. 354-55, 384-85). Papyrus Insinger (300 B.C.E.) is of two minds regarding women. They appear to the sage to be the workshops of both good and evil powers (vv. 173-74), yet for him the fear of God is also actualized in respect for women (v. 167).

2. The Figure of Personified Wisdom in the Context of the Book of Sirach

a. "All Wisdom Is From the Lord."

The programmatic title verse of the first chapter of Sirach's book reads: "All wisdom is from the Lord." Sirach 1:1-10 describes the origins and beginning of Sophia; vv. 11-13 introduce the theme of the "fear of the Lord," and vv. 14-30 establish a connection between Wisdom and the fear of the Lord by using the one to explain the other. The motifs in the first ten verses, a song of praise to Wisdom in the third person, resemble those in Prov 8:22-31 and Job 28: Wisdom comes from God, is eternally beside God, is prior to all creatures. Only God knows Wisdom and the way to her; God created her and poured her out over all creation, yet she is primarily to be found among those who fear God. In what follows, Wisdom is identified with the fear of God as its beginning (14), fullness (16), crown (18), and root (20); Wisdom is "the fear of the Lord." All thinking and action in accord with Wisdom, their beginning and ending consist in fearing the Lord (cf. also 19, 20). This Wisdom has found a dwelling place among the pious, fills the house with good things, creates peace, health, and long life. Those who desire her must keep the commandments in order to obtain wisdom from God. Of course, even before Jesus Sirach the First Testament has spoken of divine Wisdom and has shown awareness that God acts through Wisdom, teaches Wisdom to human beings, and simply *is* wise (Job 12:13; Isa 31:2), and that this Wisdom has no limits (Ps 147:5). In Prov 9:10 we even find the statement that "the fear of the LORD is the beginning of wisdom," but there it is not said in an exclusive sense. What is new in Jesus Sirach is the exclusivity, the assertion raised to the level of a slogan that all wisdom comes from God and only God is wise (1:8). This is probably a way of creating a distinction over against Greek and Hellenistic Wisdom teachings with which the Jewish population had come in contact during the second century B.C.E., teachings that did not come from the God of Israel. But it could also be the case that the author is attempting to give a new definition to Wisdom within Judaism and to defend against a broader understanding of Wisdom, perhaps even a kind of spirituality and devotion that the author found unpalatable. For Ben Sira the fear of God that is in accord with Wisdom consists in obedience to Torah, the Law. This union of Wisdom and Torah, first formulated in Deut 4:5-6 but now developed in detail for the first time, is certainly one of the great theological achievements of the Scribes,[13] but it is an act of intellectual violence that was clearly achieved at the expense of the breadth of the concept of Wisdom. Whoever follows Torah is, henceforth, a wise person. The sage studies Torah (Greek *nomos*), no longer in the comprehensive sense of instructions for living (Prov 7:2; 13:14), but in the narrower sense of the Law of Moses. In Sir 24:23 it is then explicitly said that

> All this is the book of the covenant of the Most High God,
>   the law that Moses commanded us
>   as an inheritance for the congregations of Jacob.

The abrupt statement "all this is . . . ," equating self-exalting personified Wisdom with the Torah of Moses, shows that a bit of theological acrobatics is being performed here. By this means, on the one hand, a basis is laid for a speculative grounding of Torah and the identification of the Mosaic Law with the order of the world, while on the other hand Sophia surrenders her speculative substance. For the new sages, the Scribes like Jesus Sirach, and later the rabbis who studied Torah, the joining of Wisdom to Torah was uncontested; in contrast, she never achieved a genuine foothold among the philosophers of religion in Alexandria.[14]

b. Wisdom in the Image of the Tree Goddess

The twenty-fourth chapter is the only one in the book of Sirach in which Sophia praises herself in a hymn (cf. Prov 8:22-31). We can leave aside the question whether the hymn already existed and was only edited by the author, for we can only speculate about its possible origins. It tells how Wisdom settled and put down roots in Israel, more precisely on Zion. In 24:3-6 Wisdom praises herself as an emanation from the mouth of God. She penetrates the entire creation and thrones above the cosmos, above all peoples and nations. In vv. 7-9 it is emphasized that God, the creator of the universe, also created Wisdom. God instructs her to find a dwelling-place in Israel. There is a new idea in vv. 10-11, namely that Sophia serves God in Jerusalem, on Zion—that is, in the Temple—as a liturgist and exercises her power from there. Thus the figure of Wisdom, in a manner unusual in the overall Wisdom tradition, which is more strongly international in orientation, is narrowly attached to Israel and Zion. In addition, and again quite differently from Prov 8:22-31, she is unmistakably subordinated to the God of Israel as a servant: God created her and commands her. This implicitly denies the existence of any Wisdom outside the cult administered by the priests. In this sense also there is a narrowing of the image and concept of Wisdom.

The broadly developed image of a Sophia who is rooted in the land of Israel[15] and sprouts forth multiple trees and shrubs refers to ancient religious traditions about the land. From the Middle Bronze Period (18th–15th centuries B.C.E.) onward the goddess was associated in Palestine/Israel with great trees and branches that underscored her eroticism and the powers that support life and procreation.[16] When Sir 1:20 says that "to fear the Lord is the root of wisdom, and her branches are long life" the metaphor also contains a reminiscence of the Canaanite bough-goddess (cf. Prov 3:18). Jesus Sirach may certainly have had in mind the Egyptian tree goddesses as well; we find them in tomb paintings and on papyri for the dead in the New Kingdom from the fifteenth century onward.[17] They are associated with the names of various Egyptian goddesses, but as a type they all represent a motherly, nourishing goddess who cares for the dead, providing them with shade, water, and food in the life to come (see Figure 7 in the Introduction). Jesus Sirach does not adopt the Egyptian association of the tree goddess with the realm of the dead. Sophia, in the image of the tree goddess, offers her fruits to the living, whom she invites to come to her:

> "Come to me, you who desire me,
>   and eat your fill of my fruits.
> For the memory of me is sweeter than honey,
>   and the possession of me sweeter than the honeycomb.
> Those who eat of me will hunger for more,
>   and those who drink of me will thirst for more" (Sir 24:19-21).

c. Wisdom as the Object of Male Lust

As a tree, Wisdom offers satisfaction for hunger and thirst, understood in a transferred sense, and at the same time she gives rise to new hunger and thirst (see the surpassing of this offer in John 4:10-14; 6:35; 7:37). In all this the text plays with erotic connotations, because all the Wisdom literature is fond of describing the relationship of the student of wisdom to Sophia as "desire," "imagining," "wanting to possess," and in Song 7:7-10 the man compares his beloved to a date palm that he wants to climb in order to enjoy her fruits. In Sir 6:18-31 and 51:13-30 eroticism is also an important component in the relationship of the student of wisdom to Sophia.[18] In 51:13-30 the search for Wisdom is drastically described as a burning, sexually-lustful desire on the part of the man:

> 19   . . . my hand opens her gates,
>   and I go in to her and behold her,
> 20   I have given myself entirely to her . . .
> 21   my heart is enflamed like an oven to see her,
>   therefore I have gained her as a prize possession.*

The goal that only a few reach through tireless searching for and clinging to Sophia is the presence, and indeed the possession of wisdom.

The song of praise for the good student of wisdom and Wisdom herself in 14:20–15:10 is also full of erotic allusions. Like an urgent lover or a voyeur, the student of wisdom should attempt to draw near to Sophia, even lying in wait for her. While in 42:11 this scene is in the background, as a shocking scenario intended to motivate anxious fathers to lock up their daughters, an erotic relationship with Sophia is not only permitted but even urgently recommended. In 14:26 there is an abrupt change of imagery. Previously the text spoke of the lover who pursues Sophia and pitches a tent near her house; in the next part Wisdom is again depicted in the image of the tree in which those who pursue her nest, seeking shade and shelter. That the same Wisdom approaches the people she seeks like a mother and a young bride and nourishes them with the bread of learning and the water of wisdom can be viewed as another independent image. However, we can equally well envision a connection with the tree metaphor, because the acts of the caring and loving woman who gives food and drink fit well within the ancient combination of tree and goddess.

The depiction of the relationship between the student of wisdom and Sophia in the book of Jesus Sirach is eroticized in ways that from time to time cross the line into pornography. It is true that this quasi-divine figure has erotic aspects in other Wisdom books, in her relationships both with Israel's God and with the teacher of wisdom. But when Solomon, in Wisdom 8, describes his desire for Sophia in clearly erotic images there remains a respectful distance; the greatness and a certain untouchableness of the longed-for Wisdom are maintained. In Jesus Sirach a grasping, possessive male lust is the quintessence of the metaphors.

3. Conclusion

The images of women and of Wisdom in the book of Jesus Sirach reveal convergences that grow out of the author's obvious effort to fortify the patriarchal order in house and family, in public and in the cult. The numerous texts about women do connect with older Wisdom traditions, but accent them differently. An important concern of Jesus Sirach is patriarchal control of women; his recommendations employ all means, including the theological, toward the establishment of female obedience and subordination to male authority. For this reason he attempts to nip in the bud any exchange between women that might lead to solidarity and cooperation. Women and their lives only appear in the book of Jesus Sirach through the lens of male perception. Even Sophia is described from a male perspective and in terms of male needs in the sexually-laden metaphors of the pursuit of Wisdom.

Differently from the introduction to the book of Proverbs, and differently from the Wisdom of Solomon, some 150 years later, Sophia in the book of Jesus Sirach is very clearly subordinated to the "Lord," the God of Israel, as a kind of priestly mediator. In addition, the teaching and learning of Wisdom, the love of Wisdom, is confined within a very narrow compass: Wisdom is equated with the Law of Moses and is bound to Israel and the Jerusalem Temple. A little group of Scribes has the privilege of devoting themselves to this Wisdom; the relationship to Sophia is eroticized while, at the same time, the erotic relationship between unmarried young men and women is to be controlled and, as far as possible, eliminated. The restrictions in the concept of Wisdom may represent a demarcation over against Hellenistic philosophies, but they may also have combated Jewish Wisdom traditions that displeased the author. The liveliness of such traditions, for example in the book of Wisdom and among the Therapeutes described by Philo, suggests this possibility.

NOTES

1. For text-critical questions and bibliographies listing the editions see Georg Sauer, *Jesus Sirach*. JSHRZ III, 5 (Gütersloh: Gerd Mohn, 1981), and Patrick W. Skehan and Alexander di Lella, *The Wisdom of Ben Sira*. AB 39 (New York: Doubleday, 1987). A feminist-exegetical investigation of the differences among the various text versions is a desideratum. The quoted verses follow the NRSV except where modified according to the author's translation and marked with an *.

2. In this chapter I cannot go into many of the important themes and cross-connections in and between the individual texts. See Johannes Marböck, *Weisheit im Wandel. Untersuchungen zur Weisheitstheologie bei ben Sira.* BBB 37 (Bonn: Hanstein, 1971).

3. I know of Claudia V. Camp's contribution, "Understanding a Patriarchy: Women in Second Century Jerusalem through the Eyes of Ben Sira," in Amy-Jill Levine, ed., *"Women Like This." New Perspectives on Jewish Women in the Greco-Roman World* (Atlanta: Scholars, 1991) 1–40; there is also a Th.L. dissertation by R. K. Heckelsmüller, *Jeschua Ben Sira, sein Weisheitsgedicht Kap. 24 und Spr 8—ein Vergleich* (Fribourg: Universitätsverlag, 1995).

4. Martin Hengel (*Judentum und Hellenismus* [2nd ed. Tübingen: J.C.B. Mohr (Paul Siebeck), 1973] especially at 241ff.), among others, proposes that Jesus Sirach presents his conservative Jewish positions to counter Hellenistic free thought. Marböck *(Weisheit im Wandel)* derives the reverse opinion from the same texts, namely that the author was interested in a constructive, though moderate, reception of Hellenistic ideas in Judaism.

5. Léonie J. Archer, *Her Price is Beyond Rubies. The Jewish Woman in Graeco-Roman Palestine.* JSOT.S 70 (Sheffield: Sheffield Academic Press, 1960); Amy-Jill Levine, ed., *"Women Like This";* Tal Ilan, *Jewish Women in Greco-Roman Palestine.* Texte und Studien zum Antiken Judentum 44 (Tübingen: J.C.B. Mohr [Paul Siebeck], 1995; Peabody, Mass.: Hendrickson, 1996). Cf. also, previously, Günter Mayer, *Die jüdische Frau in der hellenistisch-römischen Antike* (Stuttgart: Kohlhammer, 1987).

6. *Ben Sira's View of Women. A Literary Analysis* (Chico: Scholars, 1982).

7. *The Wisdom of Ben Sira* 90–92 and elsewhere (with further bibliography on this topic). It is unsettling to see how again and again the misogyny of this document is glossed over or even defended (thus also, for example, Maurice Gilbert, "Ben Sira et la femme," *RTL* 7 [1976] 426–42).

8. For this hermeneutic see Elisabeth Schüssler Fiorenza, *In Memory of Her. A Feminist Theological Reconstruction of Christian Origins* (New York: Crossroad, 1983) 56–60.

9. Apparently the Hebrew text still spoke of a "women's house," but a conjecture is usually offered here with the LXX.

10. For prostitutes and courtesans in the Hellenistic period see Sarah B. Pomeroy, *Goddesses, Whores, Wives, and Slaves: Women in Classical Antiquity* (New York: Schocken, 1975) 139–48.

11. These misogynistic traditions are presented in detail in Max Küchler, *Schweigen, Schmuck und Schleier. Drei neutestamentliche Vorschriften zur Verdrängung der Frauen auf dem Hintergrund einer frauenfeindlichen Exegese des Alten Testaments im antiken Judentum.* NTOA 1 (Fribourg: Universitätsverlag; Göttingen: Vandenhoeck & Ruprecht, 1986). For Jesus Sirach see especially 44–45.

12. The Egyptian texts are quoted from Helmut Brunner, *Altägyptische Weisheit. Lehren für das Leben* (Zürich and Munich, 1988).

13. On this see, in detail, the indispensable standard work of Max Küchler, *Frühjüdische Weisheitstraditionen. Zum Fortgang weisheitlichen Denkens im Bereich des frühjüdischen Jahweglaubens.* OBO 26 (Fribourg: Universitätsverlag; Göttingen: Vandenhoeck & Ruprecht, 1979), especially 38ff.; 52ff.; and Eckhard J. Schnabel, *Law and Wisdom from Ben Sira to Paul.* WUNT 2nd ser. 16 (Tübingen: Mohr, 1985).

14. Küchler, *Frühjüdische Weisheitstraditionen* 40–45.

15. It is possible that the context insinuates that Wisdom is rooted within the Temple complex. This is favored by the ancient tradition of the paradisal Temple garden (Genesis 2; Pss 52:10; 92:13; Ezek 31:1-10, and

elsewhere), taken up again in vv. 25-31 with reference to the streams (of Paradise) and the watering of the garden.

16. On this see Silvia Schroer, "Die Zweiggöttin in Palästina/Israel. Von der Mittelbronze-Zeit II B bis zu Jesus Sirach," in Max Küchler and Christoph Uehlinger, eds., *Jerusalem. Texte, Bilder, Steine*. NTOA 6 (Fribourg: Universitätsverlag; Göttingen: Vandenhoeck & Ruprecht, 1987) 218–21.

17. For the iconography of the tree goddesses see, in detail, Othmar Keel, *Das Recht der Bilder gesehen zu werden. Drei Fallstudien zur Methode der Interpretation altorientalischer Bilder*. OBO 122 (Fribourg: Universitätsverlag; Göttingen: Vandenhoeck & Ruprecht, 1992) 61–138.

18. The poem about the search for Wisdom in Sir 51:13-30 was also used in Qumran and was recorded there (see Küchler, *Schweigen, Schmuck und Schleier* 210–15); in Qumran it was in part supplied with even coarser images of male desire. The counter-image to sexualized Sophia is a dark, apocalyptic female figure who symbolizes corruption itself (4Q 184, 13; on this see Küchler, *Schweigen, Schmuck und Schleier* 192–209).

CHAPTER SEVEN

Personified Sophia in the Book of Wisdom

1. A Feminist Approach to the Figure and to the Book of Wisdom[1]

The book of Wisdom was written in Greek and is probably the last Jewish document incorporated in the Greek canon of the First Testament. It is interesting for feminist exegesis because, like other writings of the postexilic period (Proverbs 1–9; Job 28; Sirach), it speaks of personified Wisdom, a female figure who enters into the immediate presence of the God of Israel and lays claim to divinity. Traditional exegesis has thus far been unable to reach consensus about the significance of Sophia in these writings or in the religious symbol system of postexilic Israel, because such a figure is difficult to accommodate within the patriarchal concepts of a monotheistic religion. Although the influence of Egyptian and Hellenistic goddesses on the figure of Sophia has frequently been emphasized in works on the history of religions, as soon as the discussion turns to her significance within Israel and in theology scarcely any attention is paid to her femaleness. Claudia Camp in particular, in her 1985 feminist-exegetical study of the frame of the book of Wisdom, has shown us some routes that can lead us out of the old dead-end paths. She traced the relationships between the literary and historical roles of women in Israel and the Wisdom image of God and made the function of personification as a stylistic tool the starting point for her reflections. Camp's work[2] shows how important it is, methodologically speaking, for a feminist exegesis of the Wisdom writings to move from the texts to their national, social, political, cultural, and religious contexts. In addition, it has become clearer that personified Wisdom cannot be dislodged from the context of the individual Wisdom writings because she has a different function and significance in each of these documents. Thus the subject of this chapter is not limited to the rediscovery of a female image of God in Israel; instead, its purpose is to reconstruct a piece of theological history as a part of the history of Jewish women at the end of the first century B.C.E. Only when we know what significance the figure and the book of Wisdom had for Jewish women at that time, whether she advanced their oppression or their liberation from patriarchal power in society and in the religious community, will we find standpoints from which to determine whether this book is adequate to the demands of a more comprehensive liberation of women in our time.

However, the book works against just that kind of interested knowledge in the first place by deliberately seeking anonymity: by, for example, packing biblical traditions incognito in Greek-Hellenistic language, avoiding concretization, and attempting to produce the appearance of a timeless universal validity. There is to this day no consensus about the authorship of the book (is it the work of a single author or is it a collective product?). On the other hand, there is growing assent regarding its place of origin and date,[3] It seems that the book was written in Alexandria in Egypt, where many well-to-do Jews lived, and was the work of authors educated in Greek. According to Chrysostome Larcher[4] the three principal sections could have been composed successively in the last three decades before the turn of the era. The political- and social-historical background was marked by a destabilized political situation following the battle of Actium (31 B.C.E.). The situation of the Jewish communities in Egypt was deteriorating. There were many apostates, and apparently there were also defamations and persecutions within the communities themselves. In the year 30 B.C.E. Egypt became a Roman province under the control of the emperor. Influenced by these important events in world history, the book makes a deeply serious attempt to stabilize Jewish identity by attacking the apostates on the outside and at the same time strengthening the faith of loyal believers within the community. As the *Pax Romana* made itself felt in Egypt the authors raised the voice of reason, cautioning about the mortality of rulers and presenting, in the figures of Wisdom and the ideal wise king, Solomon, the indispensable preconditions for an enduring rule that would be in accord with the highest demands of intelligence and ethics. In a grand projection, the Jewish tradition is retranslated and actualized in accordance with the challenges of the time, and also explained for the sake of non-Jews.

2. Manifestations and Attributes of Sophia in Wisdom 6–10

In the first chapters of the book there is only marginal reference to Wisdom. It is above all the middle part of the book (chs. 6–8) that is devoted to personified Sophia.[5] In the introduction to his speech to the kings and tyrants of the earth (6:1-2, 9) the Wisdom teacher Solomon proclaims that he will teach Wisdom (6:9, 11, 25). When in what follows Sophia is spoken of as a female figure the non-personified meaning of wisdom (study, knowledge, experience, intelligence) is implied, even when those aspects shift into the background.

In the descriptive song in 6:12-15 Sophia is first described, much as in Proverbs 1 and 8 or Sirach 4, 6, 15, and 51, as a woman who seeks and loves those who are students of wisdom. The Wisdom teacher in 6:22-25 emphasizes explicitly that Wisdom has nothing to do with "mysteries." He will publicly proclaim her nature, her origin, make the knowledge of her public, and not (jealously) keep it for himself. According to 7:15-21 Wisdom and knowledge come from God. In Hellenism it is ultimately God who gives knowledge in all scholarly disciplines, but it is Wisdom who, as architect or constructor of all things assumes the instruction of the wise. The nature of Sophia is hymnically described in 7:22–8:1 with twenty-one epithets. Many of the statements made in this hymn about Sophia contain allusions to the ideas of Stoic philosophy and its descriptions of the divine.[6] According to this body of thought Sophia is a veil of mist, an emanation, a reflection, mirror, or image of divine reality, in some sense the dynamic-active, expressive side of the divine being. Chapter 8, with its biography of the "ideal" wise person, takes up the ideas expressed in 7:28; according to this God cannot love anyone who does not live with Wisdom. The loving relationship between Solomon and Sophia is described in highly eroticized imagery. The erotic language of these images is nothing new,[7] but what is amazing is that it is also applied to the relationship between God and Wisdom when in 8:3 Sophia is called God's lover and life-companion. The marital relationship between Sophia and God explains through illustration why she is *the* mystical possessor of divine knowledge. Her all-knowingness, not her beauty, is the motive of the wise for making her their spouse, for only Wisdom, because of her knowledge of the divine and of all things, can be the perfect counselor of a wise king (cf. Prov 8:12-16). Only her qualified counsel guarantees the young ruler fame, the ability to make just judgments, an immortal name, rule over nations, and success in war. The central section of the book reaches its climax in the prayer of the wise king in ch. 9. The sage asks God for the *paredros* (the one who sits beside the divine throne: 9:4). In religious-historical terms both the concept of the *paredros* and the image of the enthroned couple are closely connected with the divine couples in polytheistic religions (including those of Canaan and Greece). The authors show no hesitation in relying on such daring images when describing divine reality in its various aspects.

Only with the aid of Sophia can a human being recognize and fulfill the divine will (9:17). Her instruction is indispensable for human salvation. As examples of the latter ch. 10 mentions biblical stories and persons who, however, are left anonymous in order to avoid any restriction to the biblical and Jewish tradition. It is also Sophia who redeems a "holy people" (Israel) from a nation of oppressors (Egypt) (10:15-21). Thus God's saving action on behalf of Israel is retold with Sophia taking the place of the traditional name of the God who saves the ancestors of Israel and leads the Exodus. The keywords that are used here to allude to the biblical traditions are unusual. They explain the troubles (10:9, 17) of the book's addressees. In the midst of all those troubles (lapses, apostasies, fratricide, the wickedness of the nations, alienation between generations, greed, enemies, temptations, life in exile, imprisonment) Sophia brings security, wealth, success—indeed, she shows the righteous the reign of God (10:10). The memory of the Exodus assures people in distress that with the aid of Wisdom they can again resist terrible kings and that they will escape oppression in Egypt.

To formulate an interim conclusion, we may say that the femaleness of Sophia in the book of Wisdom represents not merely the erotic, but also and especially knowledge, governance, instruction, counsel, the most distinguished origin, the power to shape and to create, reliability, salvation, guidance, and virtue, especially the virtue of justice. Most of these characteristics do not fit the roles that are assigned to women in a patriarchal society.[8] All the more important, then, is the question whether there are clues here to show us why Sophia, in this female role, became a convincing religious symbol toward the end of the first century B.C.E. Is there a connection between this female image of God and the image of women, or rather women's reality, at the same time? What influences pushed Jewish men and women in Egypt toward the development of this image of God?

3. From Text to Context

The book of Wisdom contains very little direct information about women. In the fiction presented here, a male sage addresses his teaching to male rulers. Women are mentioned explicitly only in 3:12, 13, and 9:7. It is remarkable that according to 3:13-19, and contrary to ancient Israelite tradition, a woman's childlessness (like a man's) is no longer regarded as the greatest human misfortune.[9] The childless are promised fruit at the end of the ages, provided they have had no premarital or extramarital affairs. Here for the first time the First Testament tradition formulates a fundamental preference for a virtuous, freely-chosen sexual abstinence over a less-virtuous lifestyle with a wealth of children. Concretely that means that women who could not or did not desire to bear children and who voluntarily lived as virgins, single persons, or widows were accorded the same status in the religious community as married women who were mothers.[10] This unusual image of the woman who lives as a virgin and childless appears similarly in a small work of Philo of Alexandria, *De vita contemplativa.*

a. The Therapeutrides:
Jewish Women in Contemplative Communities

Philo of Alexandria (25 B.C.E. to ca. 40 C.E.) in *De vita contemplativa* describes the community of the Therapeutes (Therapeutae and Therapeutrides), who lived primarily in the vicinity of Alexandria and in their rural solitude devoted themselves to prayer, the study of Scripture, and an ascetic life.[11] The Therapeutes were "come-outers." Out of a longing for the eternal life of blessedness they abandoned life in society. Within the shelter of small settlements they led a strongly regimented common life. During the week the members spent most of their time in individual hermitages, studying and composing hymns. On the Sabbath, however, the men and women listened to a lecture together (*Vit. cont.* 32). Women were also fully integrated in the major feast of the Therapeutes, a simple but festive banquet concluding with a liturgy. In this context Philo writes (*Vit. cont.* 68) that the female members were mainly "old virgins" who freely chose to live in sexual continence. Ross S. Kraemer (1989) suggests that the "old virgins" were not only unmarried, childless women or real virgins, but also older women who had passed menopause. Interestingly, Philo gives as a reason for these women's sexual continence that they desired to live with Sophia and strive for an immortal progeny.[12] For the ascetic Therapeutes Sophia's teaching was a kind of heavenly food from which they literally tried to live (*Vit. cont.* 35). However, joyful singing and feasts were also part of this life with Wisdom. At the common night feast after the *agapē* meal the rescue of Israel at its exodus from Egypt was made present in the singing of male and female choirs. The performance concluded with a common chorus in which the men were led by the prophet Moses and the women by the prophet Miriam (*Vit. cont.* 83-84). Thus in shaping its liturgy the community paid attention to specifically female biblical traditions and included them alongside the dominant patriarchal traditions.

We may learn from *De vita contemplativa* that in Greco-Roman Egypt there were monastic Jewish groups to which certain women were admitted. The members, probably well-to-do and educated people, withdrew from their family ties in order to live together in a new spiritual family (similar to the Jesus movement). They regarded childlessness as a respected form of life, while they disdained material possessions and every kind of luxury. They rejected slavery as contrary to nature and the consequence of greed and injustice (*Vit. cont.* 70). The women living in the community were depicted by Philo as religious subjects with full equality who not only brought the awareness of their history as women into the community (Miriam)[13] but saw themselves as life-companions of divine Wisdom.

Studies of the book of Wisdom have repeatedly postulated connections with the Therapeutes. In fact there are contacts in both structure and content between the two writings that cannot be peripheral and accidental (compare, for example, *Vit. cont.* 3-9 with Wisdom 12–15). Personified Wisdom played a central role in the spirituality of the Therapeutes and in that of the authors of Wisdom. In both circles the memory of the Exodus was associated with songs of praise (Wis 10:15-21 and chs. 11–19). This Exodus is led in each case by female figures, namely the prophet Miriam or Sophia. In both circles it appears that the awareness of a special friendship with God was cultivated (Wis 7:27; *Vit. cont.* 90). Common to both is also a posture of distance toward the attitudes to life common in their environment (e.g., Wisdom 3–4) and a powerful orientation toward a divine or heavenly world and world order assumed to have been available to experience in the past and still in the present, and accepted as a certainty for the future. For the Therapeutes this worldview, of course, effected a drastic turning away from the world that cannot be demonstrated in the book of Wisdom. However, the connections are so evident that we must suppose these traditions arose in similar milieux and that there was a spiritual kinship between the two groups. Comparable examples of connections between radical "come-outer" groups and a larger circle of sympathizers who do not share the radical lifestyle but do adopt the same ideas are Qumran and the Essenes, as well as the itinerant charismatics of the Jesus movement and their non-itinerant supporters. Thus we may suppose that the book of Wisdom originated in circles in which Jewish women from Egypt/Alexandria had a strong position and in which women's religious traditions as well as a female Sophia-image of God were cultivated.[14]

b. The Power of the Goddess: Isis and Sophia

In the older Wisdom writings the figure of personified Wisdom is already strongly inspired by images and mythology of the Ancient

Near Eastern and Egyptian goddess cults. Maat, Hathor, and the tree goddesses of Egypt, but also the Syrian goddess lent their image and their power of fascination to Sophia. The observation that Sophia in the book of Wisdom is definitively shaped by the figure of Isis and the Isis theology of late Ptolemaic and early Roman Egypt was presented in a few writings as early as the first half of the twentieth century. Major publications by James M. Reese, Burton L. Mack, and John S. Kloppenborg[15] then contributed to a clearer development of the connections between Isis and Sophia.

In the late period in Egypt the cult of the goddess Isis, who according to her mythology was the sister-spouse of Osiris and mother of Horus, spread through the Aegean region and the western Mediterranean across Greece and into Italy. The Isis cult owed its popularity to the unlimited variety of the "universal goddess." Her functions, as described in the myth, of creating and protecting life as spouse and mother made her the guardian and ruler of the mystery of life. To Isis were assigned rule over the cosmic and earthly powers and over destiny, because she was not subject to the Greek goddess of ineluctable fate, Heimarmene. The Hellenistic Isis aretalogies praise the goddess as the one who gives the nations their languages, alphabets, and sciences. She is the patron of seafaring and commerce, she gives rulership to kings and validity to law, she helps those who implore her to obtain well-being and the blessing of children. Isis was honored in almost every group of the population (with the exception of the military), by men and women, but it can be demonstrated that her worship exercised a special attraction for women and probably had a positive influence on women's social position. In the aretalogies of Isis we read:

> You have made the power of women equal to that of men.

or

> It is I whom the women call goddess . . .
> I have brought woman and man together . . .
> I invented the marriage contract.[16]

Whole lists of similarities between the attributes of Isis and those of Sophia in the book of Wisdom could be drawn up, but pure motif comparisons are of little value insofar as some of these epithets are also found in hymns to other divinities (e.g., Zeus), so that a specific connection to the Isis cult cannot be demonstrated. Kloppenborg (1982) therefore attempts to present the overall theological concept that can be discerned behind the epithets and relate it to Sophia theology. He distinguishes three types of Isis worship in the first century B.C.E.: ordinary people's worship, the royal theology of the Ptolemaic and Roman kings, and that of the Greeks, as we find them in the aretalogies, in Plutarch, or in Diodorus of Sicily. While the first type scarcely influenced Alexandrian Judaism, the authors of the book of Wisdom very deliberately confronted the royal theology, and even more so the strongly missionary Isis worship of the Greeks.

The relationship between Solomon and Wisdom described at length in the central section of the book acquires an extra mythological dimension when viewed against the background of the royal Isis theology. As Solomon attains immortality through Wisdom, so Osiris and Horus attain immortality through Isis. As Sophia is both "goddess" and (desired) spouse of the king, so Isis is goddess and royal spouse, counselor and guarantor of the ruling house. She puts an end to injustice, tyranny, and wars.

In many dedicatory inscriptions Isis is praised as (universal) savior, because she has power over fate and all the cosmic forces. She is the patron of farmers, seafarers, prisoners, those who seek justice, married couples and mothers, but also of scholars. She can rescue from dangers at sea, imprisonment, and other disasters, and she helps those who honor her to attain prosperity, knowledge in all fields, professional success, and a long life. She is responsible for law and custom, gives laws and sees to it that they are obeyed, in order that all may live in peace as equals. The saving power of Sophia is described in very similar terms, especially in Wisdom 10, but also in a great many other passages; she knows how to steer a ship (10:4; 14:1-6), she comes to prisoners in their dungeons (10:13-14), she creates wealth for the righteous (3:3-6), and so on.[17]

The things said about Sophia in the book of Wisdom are thoroughly impregnated with Isis-mythologoumena; indeed, they appear to use the language of the Isis mission quite deliberately, quoting and alluding to it to sketch their picture of Sophia. Sophia is the Jewish response to the challenge of Isis- and mystery-piety in Egypt before the turn of the era. It is noteworthy that this response does not consist in negative demarcation, but in constructive integration. The book of Wisdom is addressed to Jews, and perhaps also to sympathizers with Judaism, who came into immediate contact with the worship of Isis in Alexandria, and for whom the Isis cult may have been a genuine religious alternative. Instead of demonizing Isis religion, this book attempts to set up another figure equal to Isis. The attempt reflects, on the one hand, the readiness of Judaism in Alexandria to engage with Greek culture, education, and religious practices—despite its skepticism regarding the Hellenistic world—and to orient itself within that cultural complex. On the other hand this theological complex adds something to our knowledge of a portion of women's history. Both Egyptian and Greek women in Egypt had a notable measure of legal and economic freedom. The schools of philosophy discussed the traditional roles of women.[18] Another consequence of the Hellenistic emancipation of the individual was that the exercise of religion became, in part, the responsibility of private cultic societies and was a matter of individual choice.

These changes did not pass over the Jews in Alexandria without leaving a trace. Jewish women also (at least in the upper classes) may well have attained an increasing measure of self-assurance and formulated demands to share actively in the shaping of religious life and to develop "modern" approaches to faith that could offer images of God that were appropriate to their times and appealing to their contemporaries.[19]

4. Feminist Theological Assessments

a. The Function of Personified Sophia in the Book of Wisdom

Sophia, as a personification in the book of Wisdom, combines not so much the various teachings in the Jewish tradition (as in Proverbs 1–9)[20] as the whole complex of Jewish and Greco-Hellenistic Wisdom traditions. She thus mediates between the strongly ethically-directed biblical Wisdom tradition with its interest in right order and the intellectual Wisdom conception of Greek antiquity, which in turn accompanied the philosophical-ethical search for the highest good and the greatest happiness. What the Hellenists called Philosophia, the search for Wisdom, also exists—according to the message of the book of Wisdom—in Jewish tradition. The striving after knowledge and education is regarded as a sound common feature of both cultures and the basis for an intellectual dialogue. The religious identity of the educated Jewish circles in Alexandria also proved strong enough, in time of crisis, to react to the challenges of the Hellenistic world by initiating dialogue.[21]

In Sophia, Israel's self-awareness and independence are combined with universalism and a theologically considered inculturation. This dialogue is not uncritical. Wisdom, as Jews understand her, is not a private matter and is not reserved to a few initiates in her mysteries.[22] She is the sole guarantee of the endurance of every form of dominion, because education is indispensable for just rule. Against the background of the expanding *Pax Romana,* Sophia is a symbol critical of dominion, erected against despotism and tyranny.

Wisdom appears in the image of the wise, all-knowing, just, and rescuing woman whose autonomy is both transparent to Israel's God and to the goddess Isis. Isis herself, originally an Egyptian goddess, was a religious symbol with an enormous power to create unity in the Hellenistic-Roman world. In that the figure of Sophia absorbs the mythology and theology of Isis, Egyptian Judaism sought to lend potency to its own power of integration through the use of a female divine symbol.

The significance of personified Sophia as creative of unity is also manifested in the theological structure of the book. The first part begins with the programmatic appeal: "Love righteousness, you rulers of the earth." The intention of the first part of the book is to demonstrate that, contrary to appearance, the righteous are on the better and more fruitful way, indeed that God's ordinances will ultimately command. The real world with its unjust ordinances and the striving after riches is contrasted to a just world, a counter-world whose symbolism is quite similar to the Second Testament's proposal of a "reign of God" (cf. 10:10, 14). This counter-world both exists, because it is possible to live according to its ordinances, and is utopian, because full justice will be established only by God in a "then." However, Wisdom is the teacher of righteousness accessible to all. Righteousness and Wisdom are like the outer and inner sides of a life pleasing to God. Without Wisdom there can be no just "reign of God."

b. Sophia: Symbol of Unity in Variety and Teacher of Righteousness

Sophia in the book of Wisdom is the symbol of an interreligious and intercultural dialogue in a multicultural society in the first century B.C.E. She attempts to respond positively to the existing pluralism of religions and cultures by a new interpretation of her own tradition, a ready openness to foreign influences, and acceptance of their inspiration. The "contextual theology" of the book is not afraid to speak of the God of Israel in a new language and in imagery similar to that of the goddesses. This process of reformulation, however, does not lead to a surrender of revered tradition, downgrading the independence of Jewish faith, or to esoteric syncretism. A common history lends identity "at all times and in all places" (cf. 19:22). The measuring-rod not to be surrendered throughout all the changes is God's justice. It is not for nothing that the book of Wisdom intensely opposes the service of idols and the idolatrous worship of rulers (Wisdom 11–19).

Sophia points the way to a righteous Jewish life in the midst of a pluralistic world. The fact that at that time a power to effect change was attributed to knowledge, education, and conscience is something worthy of respectful consideration especially today. In the attempt, at the end of the twentieth century, to work toward a just world order that can offer resistance to the "new world orders" of present systems of domination, experience and knowledge, especially women's wisdom, will play a very prominent role. Wisdom can rescue women; she could be the one to initiate the exodus from the complex webs of patriarchal domination. As an integrative religious symbol Sophia is well suited to create unity among religions; as a cosmopolitan symbol she can also contribute to the combating of nationalism through national identities that are open to the world.

Sophia, as an authentic biblical image of God, offers some possibilities worth considering for breaking up the rigid solidifications and ontologizing of androcentric God-language on the basis of a Jewish tradition.[23] Her attributes are God's attributes; when she speaks, God speaks; what she proclaims and does is God's will. She is the "wholly other," but she allows herself to be known. The authors of the book dared to think of Sophia within the horizon of the goddess Isis, who promises salvation because she is superior to the powers of fate. Sophia in the book of Wisdom is Israel's God in the image of a woman and a goddess.

NOTES

1. This chapter is a much-shortened version of a feminist-critical commentary on the book of Wisdom that appeared in English in Elisabeth Schüssler Fiorenza, ed., *Searching the Scriptures 2. A Feminist Commentary* (New York: Crossroad, 1994) 17–38. It has been newly translated for this volume.

2. See chapters 2 and 3 in this volume.

3. John S. Kloppenborg, "Isis and Sophia in the Book of Wisdom," *HThR* 75 (1982) 57–84; Helmut Engel, "'Was Weisheit ist und wie sie entstand, will ich verkünden,'" in Georg Hentschel and Erich Zenger, eds., *Lehrerin der Gerechtigkeit.* Erfurter Theologishe Schriften 19 (Leipzig: St. Benno, 1991) 67–102.

4. Chrysostome Larcher, *Le Libre de la Sagesse ou la Sagesse de Salomon.* EtB n.s. 1. 3 vols. (Paris: Gabalda, 1983, 1984, 1985).

5. For the structure and content of the encomium see especially Engel, "'Was Weisheit ist.'"

6. Ibid. 72–80.

7. Cf. Sir 51:13-17 and 11QPs-a XXI, 11-17.

8. See Dieter Georgi, "Frau Weisheit oder Das Recht auf schöpferische Kraft," in Leonore Siegele-Wenschkewitz, ed., *Verdrängte Vergangenheit, die uns bedrängt. Feministische Theologie in der Verantwortung für die Geschichte* (Munich: Kaiser, 1988) 225–26.

9. In fact, it seems that in the Hellenistic-Roman period great numbers of children were no longer as common, even for Jewish women, as is often supposed. Ancient documents, also from Egypt, show that a significant percentage of women had only one (surviving) child. See Günter Mayer, *Die jüdische Frau in der hellenistisch-römischen Antike* (Stuttgart: Kohlhammer, 1987) 71–76.

10. Probably 4:1-2, otherwise almost impossible to understand, also refers to such women; that is, the subject of the sentence would be "they,"

the childless, rather than "it," namely virtue. The childless are assured of immortality and the highest honor.

11. The time of composition of this work is unknown, and it is also uncertain whether Philo was making use of older or contemporary data. The comparison with the book of Wisdom is permissible, however, because the time difference cannot have been greater than fifty years.

12. In fact Philo may have composed this unusual picture of women who sought a life together with Wisdom (as their bride) under the impression that these women had already divested themselves of their femininity because of their way of life, their age, and their spiritual strivings, and had "become male," something he elsewhere describes as a spiritual goal (Ross S. Kraemer, "Monastic Jewish Women in Greco-Roman Egypt: Philo Judaeus on the Therapeutrides," *Signs. Journal of Women in Culture and Society* 14 [1989] 342–70, especially 352ff).

13. In the Hellenistic-Roman period Miriam was by far the most common name for Jewish women, in Egypt as well (Mayer, *Die jüdische Frau* 33–42).

14. In the region of Palestine there was also a famous example of a female figure in the first century B.C.E. who led a new exodus of Israel, namely Judith in the book named for her. There is an indication of the virulence of Wisdom as a female image of God in Philo's work *De fuga et inventione* 51–52 (on Gen 25:20), where, in a highly acrobatic interpretation, he on the one hand describes the nature of Wisdom as masculine and on the other hand, because of her femaleness, assigns her a rank subordinate to that of the creator of the universe. The complicated twistings should be regarded as an indication of the fact that Philo knew of Jewish groups for whom Sophia's femaleness was very important, and who certainly did *not* see Wisdom as a hypostasis subordinated to the male God or as a secondary principle (cf. Georgi, "Frau Weisheit," 249–51).

15. James M. Reese, *Hellenistic Influence on the Book of Wisdom and its Consequences.* Analecta Biblica 41 (Rome: Pontifical Biblical Institute, 1970); Burton L. Mack, *Logos und Sophia: Untersuchungen zur Weisheitstheologie im hellenistischen Judentum* (Göttingen: Vandenhoeck & Ruprecht, 1973); Kloppenborg, "Isis and Sophia."

16. The first citation is from a papyrus from Oxyrhynchus in Egypt from the second century C.E. (quoted from Bernard P. Grenfell and Arthur S. Hunt, *The Oxyrhynchus Papyri Part XI* [London: Egypt Exploration Fund, 1915] no. 1380 col. X ll. 214-15). The other quotations are from the well-known Isis aretalogy from Cyme on the coast of Asia Minor (quoted from Jan Bergmann, *Ich bin Isis. Studien zum memphitischen*

Hintergrund der griechischen Isis-Aretalogien. Acta Universitatis Upsaliensis. Historia religionum 3 [Uppsala: Universitetet; Stockholm: Almqvist & Wiksell, 1968] 301–303, ll. 10, 17, 30).

17. It is true that all these statements are related to earlier biblical traditions, but the image of personified Wisdom as savior is clearly new, since otherwise, in Israel's faith, saving activity was ascribed only to God (Deut 26:5-9; Josh 24:2-13; Pss 78, 105–106, 138; Sirach 44–50, etc.).

18. For the history of women in Hellenism see Sarah B. Pomeroy, *Goddesses, Whores, Wives, and Slaves: Women in Classical Antiquity* (New York: Schocken, 1984).

19. While the positive indications of such developments are few, the androcentric negative side evident in many early Jewish writings confirms the degree to which Jewish men were being made uncomfortable by women. They sought vehemently to eroticize biblical stories of women and to demonize female figures in order to oppose androcentric projections to the strength, knowledge, and demands of Jewish women. (Cf. Max Küchler, *Schweigen, Schmuck und Schleier. Drei neutestamentliche Vorschriften zur Verdrängung der Frauen auf dem Hintergrund einer frauenfeindlichen Exegese des Alten Testaments im antiken Judentum.* NTOA (Fribourg: Universitätsverlag; Göttingen: Vandenhoeck & Ruprecht, 1986) 192–209.

20. Cf. Claudia V. Camp, *Wisdom and the Feminine in the Book of Proverbs* (Decatur, Ga.: Almond Press, 1985) 209–25; see also Chapter 2 in this book.

21. This reaction had a certain tradition in Egyptian diaspora Judaism. The community at Elephantine took some unique paths in its worship of YHWH, also influenced by openness to religious influences in its environment, for example in the question of a *paredros* for YHWH.

22. The Septuagint translation of Job 28 and Proverbs 8 shows that there were controversies within Judaism about these questions. This translation decidedly withdraws from the openness of the older biblical Wisdom figure and makes Sophia an entity accessible only to a chosen few (cf. Max Küchler, "Gott und seine Weisheit in der Septuaginta Ijob 28; Spr 8," in Hans-Josef Klauck, ed., *Monotheismus und Christologie. Zur Gottesfrage im hellenistischen Judentum und im Urchristentum.* QD 138 (Freiburg: Herder, 1992) 118–43.

23. Early Christian groups may well have been influenced, at least indirectly, by Alexandrian Jewish Wisdom theology. Certainly they pressed the integrative function of Sophia more sharply into the realm of internal Jewish religious praxis, so that Wisdom is experienced as the host of the marginalized (cf. Chapter 8 in this book).

CHAPTER EIGHT

Jesus Sophia

Contributions of Feminist Scholarship to an Early Christian Interpretation of the Praxis and Fate of Jesus of Nazareth*

About five years ago, while I was researching the dove symbolism in Mark 1:10-11 *parr.*, I somewhat unexpectedly noticed that the Second Testament contains traces of a highly interesting early Christian "Sophialogy."[1] Suddenly I discovered that the Messiah christology and Son of Man christology were not the sole models for interpreting the earthly Jesus and "the (masculine)" Risen One; instead, the early Jewish figure of personified Wisdom had played a role as a key for understanding the Nazarene.

In my work in adult education, especially with women's groups, I have been trying for years to introduce the Wisdom image of God from the postexilic and early Jewish texts of the Bible, and also to make women more familiar with the connection between Jesus Christ and Sophia. I notice that most women have far more existential interest in the Wisdom image of God in the Bible than in Wisdom christology, the significance of which is evidently not so immediately apparent. Nevertheless, I am convinced that the Second Testament's connecting the concept of Sophia with Jesus, or "the" Christ, is theologically profitable for our Wisdom image of God and that, in turn, the figure of Jesus of Nazareth gains aspects from a Wisdom interpretation that represent a challenge to feminist theology and christology. In what follows I want to attempt to offer an introduction to the biblical bases of Sophialogy, and at the same time to describe the essentials of the status of feminist-exegetical research and its most important questions, while making no claims to exhaustiveness.[2]

1. Personified Wisdom in Postexilic and Early Jewish Texts in the Bible

It was only in the postexilic period that the figure or image of personified Wisdom *(Ḥokmā)* seems to have appeared in the circles of Wisdom teachers.[3] The oldest witness is probably Proverbs 1–9 (fifth/fourth centuries B.C.E.), followed in time by Job 28 (fifth/third centuries B.C.E.), some chapters of Jesus Sirach (second century B.C.E.), and finally the Wisdom of Solomon (end of the first century B.C.E.). It is striking that in all these writings the relationship of (Lady) Wisdom to the God of Israel is not clearly determinable. At one point we read that she was made by God or born from God before the creation and made God joyful through her high-spirited play at the time of creation (Prov 8:22-31).[4] At other times Wisdom seems to be identical with God, so that the Wisdom of Solomon can use the feminine form in telling how Wisdom led Israel out of Egypt (Wisdom 10–11). Sophia is a shifting entity, not to be systematized, representing, in a variety of images and symbols, aspects of God's goodness, kindness, and love for human beings. As creator, or co-creator with God, she shares in the formation of the world. As a prophetic teacher she appears in public places and preaches conversion to Wisdom (Proverbs 1, 8). She meets those who diligently seek knowledge and wisdom when they study; she is sister, lover, or wife to them (Wis 6:14-16). In the book of Wisdom, Sophia is even depicted as the lover of the Lord of the universe, the sharer *(paredros)* of his throne, and the mystical partner (initiate) in his knowledge (Wis 8:3; 9:4). As a host she invites into her house (Prov 9:1-5). In the old tradition of the tree goddesses of Palestine and Egypt, found in Jesus Sirach, she gives those who seek wisdom refuge and nourishment (Sir 24:19-24).[5] As a counselor she advises kings and those in power (Prov 8:14-16; Wis 8:9).

Israel's Wisdom writings must be attributed to circles within the educated upper classes. The cultural atmosphere of personified

Wisdom and those she addresses reflect that milieu of the well-to-do and influential (e.g., the invitation into a house with seven pillars in Prov 9:1, or Wisdom's closeness to kings and powerful people in Prov 8:14-16; Wisdom 6–9).

The reasons why Wisdom first appeared after the exile have by no means been adequately studied. However, Claudia Camp has indicated interesting social-historical and religious-historical backgrounds for the figure of Wisdom within the framework of the book of Proverbs. According to her findings Lady Wisdom, on the one hand, concentrates Israel's experience with wise women in a female image of God. She is an echo of the higher status of women in the period of the exile and in the early postexilic period, when they took responsibility for participating in the rebuilding of Israel. On the other hand, as mediator between God and Israel she fills the vacuum that was created by the loss of the kingship in Israel, and she takes over the king's religious functions. The place of her activity, however, is not the palace or the Temple, but the house and family.[6]

The Wisdom image of God in the book of Proverbs seems to have been a form of early Israelite monotheism that has been too little recognized and honored as an independent phenomenon. That monotheism did not hesitate to speak of the God of Israel as a female Wisdom whose images bear unmistakable features of Ancient Near Eastern goddesses (Maat, Hathor, and Syrian goddesses).[7]

The international character and openness to the world of the entire Wisdom tradition also influenced the figure of Sophia. She has inviting and integrative features; she approaches people, especially those who are especially in need of wisdom.

2. *Sophia-God and Jesus-Sophia in the Second Testament*

The traces of Wisdom traditions and a Wisdom image of God in the Second Testament were not discovered by feminist exegesis, but they received very little attention in traditional research.[8] Feminist exegesis has been more strongly interested in the Wisdom theology of the gospels, but especially in working out the central significance of Sophia christology in the first century C.E.

and attempting to bring it into conversation with current feminist theological work.

Elizabeth A. Johnson and Elisabeth Schüssler Fiorenza distinguish three stages of reflection in the Sophia theology of early Christianity, which I will here summarize through three illustrations.[9]

Very ancient[10] traditions from the Jesus movement interpret *Jesus* (or John the Baptizer and Jesus) *as emissaries of the divine Lady Wisdom.* As messenger and child of Sophia, Jesus proclaims the gospel of the poor: God Sophia is the God of the poor and the heavy-laden; all Israelites are her children. In Mark 1:9-11 *parr.* the message of the love of ("goddess") Sophia appears in the ancient symbol of the goddess of love, the dove, descending on Jesus at his baptism in the Jordan.[11] Jesus causes the poor and rejected to experience the inviting openness and kindness of Sophia by eating with toll collectors and sinners (toll collectors, prostitutes, sinners of both sexes). Schüssler Fiorenza suggests that the *Sitz im Leben* of the saying about Wisdom being justified by *all* her children (Luke 7:35) is this common table with the rejected of society.

> (And all the people who heard this,
> including the tax collectors, acknowledged the justice of God,
> because they had been baptized with John's baptism.
> But by refusing to be baptized by him, the Pharisees and the lawyers
> rejected God's purpose for themselves.)
> "To what then will I compare the people of this generation,
> and what are they like?
> They are like children sitting in the marketplace
> and calling to one another,
>   'We played the flute for you, and you did not dance;
>   we wailed, and you did not weep.'
> For John the Baptist has come
> eating no bread and drinking no wine,
> and you say, 'He has a demon';
> the Son of Man has come eating and drinking,
> and you say, 'Look, a glutton and a drunkard,
> a friend of tax collectors and sinners!'
> Nevertheless, wisdom is vindicated by all her children" (Luke 7:29-
>   35; cf. Matt 11:16-19).

The Jesus movement and the young Church also found that the prophets of Wisdom were persecuted and killed:

> "Therefore I send you prophets, sages, and scribes,
> some of whom you will kill and crucify,
> and some you will flog in your synagogues
> and pursue from town to town . . .
> Jerusalem, Jerusalem,
> the city that kills the prophets
> and stones those who are sent to it!
> How often have I desired to gather your children together
> as a hen gathers her brood under her wings,
> and you were not willing!
> See, your house is left to you, desolate" (Matt 23:34-38).

It is clear from the fact that the evangelist lets the key word "crucify" slip into this saying that Jesus, as the (last) prophet of Sophia, shared the fate of all her emissaries, and that the same fate threatened Jesus' followers. The death of Jesus is given a Wisdom interpretation as the consequence of his praxis of gathering the children of Israel under the wings of Sophia-God.

The loving-caring or inviting-open image of Sophia-God is also reflected in parables in the gospels of Matthew and Luke.[12] The parable of the man (or king) who invites people to a great feast or wedding feast (Luke 14:15-24 *par.* Matt 22:1-10) and who, because all the guests excuse themselves, sends his servants into the streets so that the banquet hall may be filled, borrows from the Wisdom motif of Sophia's invitation. In Prov 9:1-5 she invites to a meal in her house. She sends her maidservants to the high places in the city to call the simple and those without sense. She invites to the way of life, while Folly entices people into Sheol.

However, Luke's and Matthew's common source (Q, the Sayings Source) tells the parable of Sophia's invitation in purely patriarchal images. What remains is the idea of a God—in the parable a king, a man—who has invited certain people to a feast, but who ultimately allows the poor and marginalized to share in the joy of the meal. In Matthew's version the servants of the king, like the messengers of Wisdom (Matt 23:34), even die a violent death. Luke skillfully inserts the well-known parables of the lost into the context of meal companionship with sinners (Luke 15). Thus in the parable of the lost coin God's attitude is indirectly, but very clearly, compared with the attitude of a woman seeking. The motherly Sophia-God gathers her children, her chicks, the lost sheep, the valuable coin, the lost sons.

In other—simultaneous or later—theological steps *the Risen One or the earthly Jesus is identified with Sophia.* Paul, in 1 Corinthians, reacts against a Wisdom theology or christology of the (pre-Pauline) missionary movement that confesses the Risen One, Christ, as "the power of God and the wisdom of God" (1 Cor 1:24; cf. 1:30; 2:7; 10:1-32). A series of pre-Pauline hymns also praise the universal and cosmic lordship of the Risen One in the language of Jewish-Hellenistic Sophia theology and of the Isis cult (Phil 2:6-11; 1 Tim 3:16; Col 1:15-20; Eph 2:14-16; Heb 1:3; 1 Pet 3:18; John 1:1-14). Like Sophia (1 Enoch 42:1-2), Jesus Christ found no dwelling-place on earth and was therefore exalted by God as *Kyrios* over the whole world.

This cosmic Sophialogy fell victim later, in Christian Gnosticism,[13] to the danger that was being combated even before Paul, namely an "emptying of the cross" (1 Cor 1:17), that is, the neglect of the memory of the life and death of Jesus in favor of a strongly mythological, spiritualizing, and in its tendency imperial "Ruler of the World" theology. In contrast, where there are traces of an identification of Jesus with Sophia in the gospels the idea of incarnation is more powerfully in the foreground. Like personified Wisdom, Jesus teaches in Mark 6:30–8:21,[14] but the earthly Jesus is more than the fabled wisdom of Solomon (Matt 12:42 *par.* Luke 11:31), whom the Queen of the South came from the ends of the earth to seek, for Jesus is himself the incarnate Sophia whose yoke is light, as described in Sir 6:28-31 and 51:26-27.

> "I thank you, Father,
> Lord of heaven and earth,
> because you have hidden these things from the wise and the
>   intelligent
> and have revealed them to infants;
> yes, Father, for such was your gracious will.

All things have been handed over to me by my Father;
and no one knows the Son except the Father,
and no one knows the Father except the Son
and anyone to whom the Son chooses to reveal him.
Come to me, all you that are weary and are carrying heavy burdens,
and I will give you rest.
Take my yoke upon you, and learn from me;
for I am gentle and humble in heart,
and you will find rest for your souls.
For my yoke is easy,
and my burden is light (Matt 11:25-29).

In the Sayings Source this text already bears a clear overlayer of masculine Logos/Son metaphors (see further below). The author of the gospel of Matthew allows the identification of Jesus with Sophia to remain obvious and makes various uses of it also in anti-Jewish statements because Sophia is rejected by *her* people.

In the Fourth Gospel both the earthly Jesus and the preexistent Christ are identified with Sophia in a variety of metaphors and speeches. Thus Jesus, like *Ḥokmā* (Proverbs 1, 8) stands up and cries aloud (John 7:28-29) as a teacher, and proclaims the teachings of Wisdom (John 8:23-24; 12:44-48; cf. also Sir 24:1-22) in first-person speeches, as *Ḥokmā* proclaims herself. As in Wisdom of Solomon Sophia and God are in intimate relationship, so the Fourth Gospel emphasizes the intimacy of Father and Son (John 5:19-22). Wherever Jesus describes himself as the water and bread of life (John 4:10-14; 6:30-35; 7:37) he enters into the inheritance of the tree goddess Sophia, who in Sirach 24 invites all to be filled with her fruits. Jesus, however, offers more than Wisdom (John 6:35), who in Sir 24:21 promises that "those who eat of me will hunger for more, and those who drink of me will thirst for more."

The metaphors of light, life, seeking, and finding also lead us repeatedly to texts from postexilic Wisdom theology. Central to the Wisdom christology of the Fourth Gospel is the Prologue, which praises Jesus as the preexistent and incarnate Logos. While the source of the motifs is clearly in the Wisdom tradition (cf. especially Prov 8:22-31), the evangelist already, and steadily, uses the masculine concept of the Logos in place of the conceptual language of

Sophia. Scholars are generally in agreement now that this dilution of the Sophia terminology in the Second Testament sources was influenced by Philo of Alexandria. He constructed a complex philosophical and theological system within which the male Logos absorbed the female Sophia (for clearly patriarchal reasons) and so brought about her disappearance.[15]

3. The *Sitz* im Leben *of Jesus-Sophia Theology*

Elisabeth Schüssler Fiorenza, following Felix Christ and others, posits that Sophia-God was already connected with the God of the poor and the gospel for the poor in the Jewish tradition. She sees the *Sitz im Leben* of the identification of the earthly Jesus with Sophia in people's experience of Jesus as one who shared meals with the poor and ostracized in Israel, whereby the gracious openness and love of Sophia for all her children was made visible; indeed, in Jesus, Sophia-God herself could be experienced among human beings.

Recently Luise Schottroff, in a feminist analysis of the Sayings Source,[16] has strenuously objected to the supposition that there was a connection between Sophia-God and the gospel for the poor. Because her challenges to feminist research to date on Sophia christology are very deep-seated, her principal arguments need to be presented here.

Schottroff asserts, to begin with, that in the postexilic and early Jewish Wisdom writings the gospel for the poor plays no part at all, and that these writings instead address a *paterfamilias* from the well-to-do classes and offer him directions for a life of wisdom. In contrast, she finds that, given its origins, the tradition of the gospel for the poor is clearly prophetic. Against Schüssler Fiorenza and others, Schottroff thus does not recognize Matt 11:25, 28-30 as genuine Wisdom texts, because in this new context the fragments of Wisdom teaching are placed in service of the prophetically-shaped gospel for the poor. Thus the rejection of Jesus' emissaries is also not to be compared with the rejection of Sophia, because Jesus' emissaries are killed, while Sophia withdraws unmolested into heaven. Schottroff radically questions the starting point of the work to date toward development of a feminist Sophia theology. For her it is not the allusions to Sophia that form the historically and theologically convincing starting point for a feminist Wisdom christology or theology, but the fact that the gospel of the poor, the revelation of God to the little ones, the un-educated (Greek *nepioi*), is a women's gospel, because women, more often than men, were counted among the "minors" and the uneducated.

> The election of the minors, the poor, and children by God meant, in the praxis of an androcentrically-thinking Jesus movement, the opening of their eyes to the fate of women and the encouraging of women toward independent action in the awareness that they were daughters of God. Further development from that starting point through the overcoming of the androcentrism of the synoptic tradi-tion can open eyes still more to a justice that omits no one and makes no victims invisible, and that will effect the liberation of women. The critique presented here of the concept of a feminist Sophia theology or Sophia christology has historical and theological bases as well. The historical ground is the assessment of the Wisdom tradition, which is by no means oriented to the goal of universal jus-tice. The theological ground is the significance of the connection be-tween the gospel for the poor and justice and liberation for women.[17]

I want to offer some points for consideration and open ques-tions in response to this critique by Luise Schottroff, which I think is very important. They are conceived as impulses for a profes-sional discussion that needs to be pursued still farther, and for his-torical research.

1. The Wisdom literature of the postexilic and early Jewish pe-riod is certainly in large part patriarchal and belongs to the upper classes. Nevertheless, the results of Claudia Camp's work and that of Athalya Brenner indicate that the frame of the book of Proverbs is woman-oriented, and that possibly the teachings found there were even handed on from mother to son.[18] In terms of content we find here the teaching of Wisdom, which, however, very explicitly includes the ancient Israelite concept of "right order." It is not true that Wisdom is not interested in questions of universal justice. The central struggle in the book of Job, for example, is over the ques-tion of justice.[19] Certainly the Wisdom and prophetic circles come

into contact primarily in relation to analysis of the reasons for injustice (cf., for example, Job 24 and Sir 34:21–35:26). As for practical consequences, in taking the part of the disadvantaged prophecy proceeds to protests, public social criticism, accusation, suing for justice for the poor. Wisdom is often content to appeal to those who have wealth not to surrender themselves to greed for profit (Prov 3:27-35; 8:10-21) and not to exploit the poor among their people.

2. It is questionable whether Jewish Wisdom in the first century C.E. was still only an interest of the upper classes. In my opinion Max Küchler has persuasively demonstrated, with a great deal of evidence, that "the claim to possession of wisdom was character-istic of *all* early Jewish confessional groups," and in fact that in Palestine at that time a positively "sapiential milieu" reigned supreme.[20] The Wisdom tendencies in the gospels allow us to con-clude to a tradition of popular wisdom, and perhaps there were in-deed poor people who went to the synagogues and public squares to listen to teachings about Wisdom, as when they listen to Jesus in Nazareth and then ask: "Where did this man get all this? What is this wisdom that has been given to him? What deeds of power are being done by his hands!" (Mark 6:2 *par.* Matt 13:54).

It seems certain to me, at least, that Wisdom, prophetic, and apocalyptic thought had, by the first century, exercised a strong mutual influence for a long time, and that those traditions of thought shaped the most widely diverse groups. Thus Philo of Alexandria writes in his *De vita contemplativa* about the Thera-peutes, a group who lived far from the turmoil of the cities, highly ascetic in their lifestyle and nourished only by the food of Wis-dom. These groups took Sophia's feeding (Prov 9:1-4; Sir 24:21) literally as a study (§35) that men and women could pursue sepa-rately, but with full equality. At the common banquets all cele-brated together, and there were no slaves to serve at table. Wisdom ideas must therefore have seized strongly on the most diverse groups, and they apparently had the power to build community.[21]

3. Despite Luise Schottroff's objections I am convinced that the *Sitz im Leben* of the synoptics' Sophia theology was Jesus' open practice of community meals, the invitation extended by Sophia-God to the poor and the marginalized. It is true that the connecting

thread between preaching to those who do not understand (Prov 1:22; 9:4, and elsewhere) and openness to those who exist on the margins is thin; this I admit. But early Christianity, with its Messiah christology, of course also attached some highly significant changes in the Jewish messianic concepts of the first century C.E. to very thin threads. Jesus was not the anticipated triumphalist messianic figure—whether the expectations were political or religious. He established no kingship, had no ruling power, did not succeed in setting up right and justice in the land. John's question, "Are you the one who is to come, or are we to wait for another?" (Luke 7:19) reflects doubt—a doubt that could not be more obvious—about whether Jesus was the Messiah at all. And yet the Christians of that time held fast to the identification of Jesus as Messiah, and initiated a radical reinterpretation of the messianic title. To that extent it is possible that Wisdom traditions and Wisdom images of God were also newly filled with the prophetic aims of justice and God's partisanship for the oppressed, and that they were in fact reinterpreted as well. Now it is not the simple whom Sophia invites to her palace; she invites the poor to her meal. Now the yoke laid on people is not that of hard study, but the yoke of oppression. Now the rejection of Wisdom does not simply result in her withdrawal and exaltation, but in her crucifixion, death, and exaltation and that of her messengers.

4. Perspectives of a Feminist Sophia Christology

Is it possible to think that Jewish Wisdom theology experienced its most profound alteration and variation at the hands of Christian groups and communities, that Sophia-God was connected with a historical person, the Jew Jesus of Nazareth, became incarnate in him, and through that incarnation acquired a political and social dimension and thus became the gospel for the poor? Preexistent Sophia becomes human, suffers violence, is rejected, killed, and exalted to God, whence at the end of time she will return.

If this Sophia christology of the cross can be historically demonstrated, it can provide a solid foundation for a feminist spirituality and christology that does not drift off into spiritualization, esotericism, and Gnosticism, but holds fast to the gospel of Sophia-God,

who in Jesus came to the poorest of this world, including especially women and children, but also to all who are discriminated
against because of the color of their skin, and shared their fate.
This gospel is also the message that God enters entirely into her/
his suffering creation. Under the precondition that the theologically central idea of suffering Sophia is not abandoned in favor of
a purely heavenly-lovely image of God, it seems to me that a
Sophialogy can truly be a challenging way for a future feminist
christology to go. Sophia-God became human in the man Jesus.
But the Risen One is Christ, is Sophia, is neither male nor female,
just as God cannot be grasped in our categories of man and woman.
We can thus speak of God as both Father and Sophia.[22] The doctrine of the Trinity, which attempts to formulate the idea that even
the one God only lives and is conceivable as in personal relationship, is open to the femaleness of the third divine person, Sophia.

The traces of Wisdom christology in the Second Testament are
not a finished theological system; they must be developed and, in
part, critically revised. Thus we must take care that we do not
adopt the anti-Jewish implications of a Matthean or Johannine
Wisdom christology. The rejection of Sophia must not be ascribed
to the Jewish people and thus lead to another theory of God(dess)-
murder.[23] We must take care that Sophia does not become another
middle-class goddess at our hands. And it is our duty to speak of
the crucified Sophia, not to fall victim to new life-hating theories
of sacrifice, but in order to recall, in dangerous memories, the suffering of our sisters and mothers in faith, how they were forgotten
and suppressed. Sophia-God shares the suffering of the oppressed
women and men of this world and the suffering of the exploited
creation; in Jesus she shared their death. But she overcame death
and is Mistress of the whole world.

NOTES

* The volume edited by Doris Strahm and Regula Strobel, *Vom Verlangen nach Heilwerden: Christologie in feministisch-theologischer Sicht*
(Fribourg: Exodus, 1991) is one of the most important feminist theologi-

cal books of recent years. The following year the journal *Orientierung* published a critical review by Dorothee Sölle, in which she dismissed in a single sentence my attempt at a Wisdom approach to Jesus, or rather to Christ: "Wisdom has nothing to do with the prophetic tradition, and talk of a 'crucified' Sophia not only de-historicizes Jesus but serves to advance the depoliticization of the white middle-class woman still further" (ibid. 131). Many readers felt that this remark was an unjustified piece of sarcasm, because the critical points in the article were presented quite openly and with considerable subtlety. Nevertheless, this sharp remark initiated a constructive conflict. Dorothee Sölle was able to explain her point of view at a meeting with feminist theologians in Zürich. In January 1995 Luise Schottroff and I continued the dispute over this theme in a very productive way. Luise Schottroff's position on Sophia christology can be found in her essay on Q (see the bibliographical list below).

The fruit of our discussion is for me (beyond what was already formulated in the essay itself) summarized in the following points:

1. I am more certain than ever that the controversy is, among other things, confessionally based. Elisabeth Schüssler Fiorenza and I, as Catholic women, have no hesitation in working with Wisdom texts and making theological use of them. In the cases of Dorothee Sölle and Luise Schottroff I recognize a very deep-rooted—and I think typically Protestant—aversion to Wisdom literature. The idea that Wisdom has nothing at all to do with prophecy (see above) is simply a prejudice. Texts in the book of Job (Job 24), Jesus Sirach (34:24-27), and Wisdom of Solomon (Wisdom 2) yield nothing in the sharpness of their social analysis and language to many prophetic texts. In addition, I consider it highly problematic to permit only the prophetic tradition (for Schottroff the Gospel of the Poor) validity as a basis for feminist theologies, because that represents a narrowing of the pluralism existing in the Israelite and Jewish tradition, which has preserved Law, Wisdom (writings) and prophecy, and in which prophecy does not simply rise above everything else. Judaism has brought the most varied traditions into conversation in very innovative ways, so that, for example, Jewish midrash on Torah can start from the ideas of Qoheleth. I suspect that behind this narrowing tendency is some late influence of dialectical theology and of Barthianism, for whose vertical understanding of revelation prophecy alone suffices, while all natural, humanly transmitted Wisdom teachings and laws are not to be considered as conclusive divine revelation.

2. I admit that Luise Schottroff is right, in part, in being skeptical about the *Sitz im Leben* of the Wisdom writings. All the Wisdom texts are literature of the upper classes, and some are clearly interested in strengthening

Israelite patriarchy—especially, of course, Jesus Sirach. The "book of Wisdom" (see my essay on this subject in Elisabeth Schüssler Fiorenza, ed., *Searching the Scriptures 2: A Feminist Commentary* [New York: Crossroad, 1994] 17–38) is, however, such a striking counter-example that it is simply not right to dismiss Wisdom literature *a priori* as patriarchal. The traditions of Israel's writing prophets cannot be spared from the feminist criticism that they were written by highly educated people. The theological nodal points in the work of a Hosea or Ezekiel have, as feminist exegesis itself has shown, in many ways advanced patriarchal ideas and structures in society and religion. The hermeneutics of suspicion are a *conditio sine qua non* for our feminist work. However, they must not prevent us from engaging in conversation with the content of these writings; on the contrary, they should keep us at the task because otherwise parts of women's history will be lost.

3. Luise Schottroff's critique in particular stands as a warning signal for my work: danger! traps! Feminist Wisdom theology must be anchored in a more comprehensive theology of justice and partisanship for the weakest, because otherwise it really can be misused in our context. We must hold fast to the justice for which Wisdom intervenes, as well as the prophetic aspects it always had. In this sense I am happy to agree with Paul, who holds up the cross as a critique of every kind of Wisdom teaching (1 Corinthians 1–2).

In her book *Jesus: Miriam's Child, Sophia's Prophet: Critical Issues in Feminist Christology* (New York: Continuum, 1994) Elisabeth Schüssler Fiorenza has developed the christology of Wisdom's emissary more fully than anyone else. She holds fast to the necessity of releasing our talk about God and Christ from its dangerous gender fixations by means of the Wisdom tradition. That the biblical texts, and especially their metaphorical language and reflective mythology contain many potential discoveries and impulses corresponds to my own conviction and is an important reason for not surrendering these traditions, despite all the criticism we may receive.

Literature:

Elisabeth Schüssler Fiorenza, *Jesus: Miriam's Child, Sophia's Prophet. Critical Issues in Feminist Christology* (New York: Continuum, 1994).

Luise Schottroff, "The Sayings Source Q," in Elisabeth Schüssler Fiorenza, ed., *Searching the Scriptures 2: A Feminist Commentary* (New York: Crossroad, 1994) 510–34.

Dorothee Sölle, "Zwischen Patriarchat, Antijudaismus und Totalitarianismus. Anmerkungen zu einer Christologie in feministisch-theologischer Sicht," *Orientierung* 56 (1992) 130–33.

The connection between Jesus or Christ and ideas about Wisdom has meanwhile—thanks to the impulse given by feminist discussions—become the object of numerous studies by male authors. The following references make no claim to completeness:

> Hermann von Lips, "Christus als Sophia? Weisheitliche Traditionen in der urchristlichen Christologie," in Cilliers Breytenbach and Henning Paulsen, eds., *Anfänge der Christologie. Festschrift für Ferdinand Hahn* (Göttingen: Vandenhoeck & Ruprecht, 1991) 75–95.

> Martin Scott, *Sophia and the Johannine Jesus.* JSOT.S 71 (Sheffield: JSOT Press, 1992).

1. See Silvia Schroer, "The Spirit, Wisdom, and the Dove," Chapter 8 in this book. In what follows I will use both the concepts of "Sophialogy" and "Sophia christology." There is a difficulty here, because Sophialogy is a very academic and unwieldy concept, while "Sophia christology" is easier to understand because it contains the Christ-title. The confession that Jesus is the Christ (the Messiah, the Anointed), however, rests on a different tradition in thought than does the identification of Jesus-Sophia. Nevertheless, the Christ-title has been and is so dominant in Christian tradition that there is scarcely any possibility within our languages to speak in any other way about "the" Exalted or Risen One.

2. Let me mention in advance the feminist publications on which my remarks are based; they are indispensable and highly recommended for anyone who wants to go deeper into this whole body of material. Standard works of classical exegesis on the various themes may be found in the works cited. I can refer only briefly to details in the professional discussions of the topics through references in the notes. The subtle argumentation and lines of proof for positions that I can only sketch here should be sought in the following publications: Elizabeth A. Johnson, "Jesus, The Wisdom of God. A Biblical Basis for Non-Androcentric Christology," *EThL* 61 (1985) 261–94; Susan Cady, Marian Ronan, and Hal Taussig, *Sophia. The Future of Feminist Spirituality* (San Francisco: Harper & Row, 1986); Elisabeth Schüssler Fiorenza, *In Memory of Her. A Feminist Theological Reconstruction of Christian Origins* (New York: Crossroad, 1983); eadem, "Auf den Spuren der Weisheit," in Verena Wodtke-Werner, ed., *Auf den Spuren der Weisheit. Sophia: Wegweiserin für ein neues*

Gottesbild (Freiburg: Herder, 1991); Luise Schottroff, "Wander-prophetInnen. Eine feministische Analyse der Logienquelle," *EvTh* 51 (1991) 332–44.

3. I can refer only summarily to the feminist literature on postexilic and early Jewish Wisdom literature: Claudia Camp, *Wisdom and the Feminine in the Book of Proverbs* (Decatur, Ga.: Almond, 1985); Dieter Georgi, "Frau Weisheit oder das Recht auf Freiheit als schöpferische Kraft," in Leonore Siegele-Wenschkewitz, ed., *Verdrängte Vergangenheit, die uns bedrängt* (Munich: Kaiser, 1988) 243–76; Silvia Schroer, "Wise Women and Counselors in Israel: Models for Personified *Ḥokmā,*" Chapter 3 in this volume; eadem, "Divine Wisdom and Postexilic Monotheism," Chapter 2 in this volume. There is a simple introduction to the biblical figure of Wisdom in the issue entitled "Sophia. Gott im Bild einer Frau," *Bibel heute* 103 (1990) 146–63.

4. On this see Othmar Keel, *Die Weisheit spielt vor Gott. Ein ikonographischer Beitrag zur Deutung der meṣaḥäqät in Sprüche 8,30f* (Fribourg: Universitätsverlag; Göttingen: Vandenhoeck & Ruprecht, 1974) 12–13.

5. Cf. Silvia Schroer, "Die Zweiggöttin in Palästina/Israel. Von der Mittelbronze-Zeit II B bis zu Jesus Sirach," in Max Küchler and Christoph Uehlinger, eds., *Jerusalem. Texte, Bilder, Steine*. NTOA 6 (Fribourg: Universitätsverlag; Göttingen: Vandenhoeck & Ruprecht, 1987) 201–25.

6. For this paragraph see Claudia Camp, *Wisdom and the Feminine,* and Silvia Schroer, "Divine Wisdom and Postexilic Monotheism," Chapter 2 in this volume.

7. See the groundbreaking work of Urs Winter, *Frau und Göttin. Exegetische und ikonographische Studien zum weiblichen Gottesbild im Alten Israel und dessen Umwelt*. OBO 53 (Fribourg: Universitätsverlag; Göttingen: Vandenhoeck & Ruprecht, 1983), especially 508–29; Bernhard Lang, *Wisdom and the Book of Proverbs. An Israelite Goddess Redefined* (New York: Pilgrim, 1986); Christa Bauer-Kayatz, *Studien zu Proverbien 1–9*. WMANT 22 (Neukirchen-Vluyn: Neukirchener Verlag, 1966) 75–95. For what follows see Silvia Schroer, "Divine Wisdom and Postexilic Monotheism," above.

8. We may mention the following selected works: Ulrich Wilckens, *Weisheit und Torheit. Eine exegetisch-religionsgeschichtliche Untersuchung zu 1 Kor 1 und 2*. BHTh 26 (Tübingen: Mohr, 1959) 145–59; Felix Christ, *Jesus Sophia. Die Sophia-christologie bei den Synoptikern*. AThANT 57 (Zürich: Zwingli, 1970); Elisabeth Schüssler Fiorenza, "Wisdom, Mythology, and the Christological Hymns of the New Testament," in Robert L. Wilken, ed., *Aspects of Wisdom in Judaism and Early*

Christianity (Notre Dame and London: University of Notre Dame Press, 1975) 17–42; James M. Robinson, "Jesus as Sophos and Sophia: Wisdom-Tradition and the Gospels," in ibid. 1–16; Max Küchler, *Frühjüdische Weisheitstraditionen. Zum Fortgang weisheitlichen Denkens im Bereich des frühjüdischen Jahweglaubens.* OBO 26 (Fribourg: Universitätsverlag; Göttingen: Vandenhoeck & Ruprecht, 1979).

9. Cf. Elizabeth A. Johnson, "Jesus, The Wisdom of God," and especially Elisabeth Schüssler Fiorenza, "Auf den Spuren der Weisheit."

10. Schüssler Fiorenza even suggests that these are the oldest traditions. However, since we are in the realm of historical reconstructions and models, I prefer a more cautious formulation. Their great significance is not to be dismissed, with or without a primacy in time.

11. See the bibliography in note 1.

12. To my knowledge the traces of Wisdom images of God in the parables of the Second Testament have not been thoroughly investigated.

13. For Sophia in Gnosticism cf. the following: Elaine Pagels, *The Gnostic Gospels* (New York: Random House, 1979); Dieter Georgi, "Zum Wesen der Weisheit nach der 'Weisheit Salomos,'" in Jacob Taubes, ed., *Gnosis und Politik.* Religionstheorie und Politische Theologie 2 (Munich and Paderborn: W. Fink, 1984) 66–81; Deirdre J. Good, *Reconstructing the Tradition of Sophia in Gnostic Literature.* SBL Monograph Series 32 (Atlanta: Scholars, 1987); Karen L. King, ed., *Images of the Feminine in Gnosticism* (Philadelphia: Fortress, 1988).

14. See the interesting article by Hugh M. Humphrey, "Jesus as Wisdom in Mark," *BTB* 19 (1989) 48–53.

15. For the Fourth Gospel see especially Cady, Ronan, and Taussig, *Sophia;* Schüssler Fiorenza, *In Memory of Her;* and Silvia Schroer, "Die Zweiggöttin," 221. The proof that the idea of a preexistent Messiah is of Wisdom origin was given by Gottfried Schimanowski, *Weisheit und Messias.* WUNT 2nd ser. 17 (Tübingen: J.C.B. Mohr [Paul Siebeck], 1985). For the conceptual language of Logos and Sophia see Burton L. Mack, *Logos und Sophia. Untersuchungen zur Weisheitstheologie im hellenistischen Judentum.* StUNT 10 (Göttingen: Vandenhoeck & Ruprecht, 1973). For the whole further development of Wisdom theology in Gnosticism, in the Church Fathers, and in the mysticism of, for example, Hildegard of Bingen, we can here refer only summarily to the brief remarks in Cady, Ronan, and Taussig, *Sophia* 55–64, and to Verena Wodtke-Werner, ed., *Auf den Spuren der Weisheit.* There are traces of a very early tendency to subordinate Sophia by identifying her with the Church or with Mary (cf. also my essay cited in n. 1 above, and Helen Schüngel-Straumann, "Alttestamentliche Weisheitstexte als marianische

Liturgie," in Elisabeth Gössmann and Dieter R. Bauer, eds., *Maria: für alle Frauen oder über allen Frauen?* [Freiburg: Herder, 1989] 12–35).

16. See Luise Schottroff, "Wanderprophetinnen;" eadem, "Armut," *NBL* 1:173–74.

17. Schottroff, "Wanderprophetinnen," 343.

18. This interesting thesis was presented by Athalya Brenner and Fokkelien van Dijk-Hemmes at the international meeting of the Society of Biblical Literature in Vienna, August 1990, in their paper "On Gendering Biblical Texts."

19. Cf. Silvia Schroer, "Entstehungsgeschichtliche und gegenwärtige Situierungen des Hiob-Buches," in Ökumenischer Arbeitskreis für Bibelarbeit, ed., *Hiob* (Basel and Einsiedeln: EOS, 1989), especially 46–62.

20. Max Küchler, *Frühjüdische Weisheitstraditionen,* especially 13–30, at 15.

21. For the Therapeutes see Dieter Georgi, "Frau Weisheit," 253–59. Georgi supposes that behind the Wisdom of Solomon stood communities similar to the Therapeutes. It seems to me especially interesting that the Therapeutes were fundamentally convinced of the equality of all people "by nature." Thus Philo writes: "They do not use the ministrations of slaves, looking upon the possession of servants or slaves to be a thing absolutely and wholly contrary to nature, for nature has created all [people] as free, but the injustice and covetousness of some . . . who prefer inequality, that cause of all evil, having subdued some, has given to the more powerful authority over those who are weaker" (*De vita contemplativa* §70; translation from C. D. Yonge, *The Works of Philo. Complete and Unabridged* (new updated ed. Peabody, Mass.: Hendrickson, 1993). Apparently, then, even in ascetic and rather esoteric communities that devoted themselves entirely to Wisdom there was the possibility of a strong awareness of greater righteousness, although in this case it was founded on philosophy and natural law, not on the Bible. Unfortunately I cannot go more fully here into the interesting connections between Isis theology and Sophia theology, which can be demonstrated from the time of Wisdom of Solomon and, according to Schüssler Fiorenza, in the period of the Second Testament. See, among others, the important article by John S. Kloppenborg, "Isis and Sophia in the Book of Wisdom," *HThR* 75 (1982) 57–84.

22. Here I want to emphatically support the initiative of Elisabeth Schüssler Fiorenza in "Auf den Spuren der Weisheit." She suggests that we "shift the discussion about the female figure of Wisdom from the psychological-ontological-christological level to the linguistic-theological

level" (against Christa Mulack, but also against Elizabeth A. Johnson), in order that Wisdom christology not lead to ontological consolidation of the culturally-conditioned concepts of "masculine" and "feminine." The Wisdom theology of Proverbs can be regarded as an attempt to speak of Israel's God in female images, and indeed *within* a monotheistic symbol system.

23. For discussion see the collected volume edited by Leonore Siegele-Wenschkewitz, *Verdrängte Vergangenheit, die uns bedrängt* (Munich: Kaiser, 1988). The thesis that Israelite or Jewish patriarchy and monotheism had the goddess in Israel on their conscience has no historical basis. The great goddesses of the Canaanite period had disappeared in Palestine as early as the Late Bronze Period, that is, before there was any such thing as a people or state of Israel.

CHAPTER NINE

The Spirit, Wisdom, and the Dove:
Feminist-Critical Exegesis of a Second Testament Symbol Against the Background of Its History in Ancient Near Eastern and Hellenistic-Early Jewish Tradition*

1. The Dove at Jesus' Baptism: An Ambiguous Symbol?

All four gospels tell, in connection with Jesus' baptism in the Jordan, of the appearance of the Spirit in the form of a dove that descends on Jesus accompanied by a voice: "You are my Son, the Beloved; with you I am well pleased" (Mark 1:11). The versions in the four gospels differ in small but important details.[1] In Mark 1:10-11 the appearance of the dove is narrated as Jesus' visionary experience: after being baptized he sees the heavens open and the Spirit *(to pneuma)* "like a dove" *(hōs peristeran)* descending, and hears *(eis auton,* "within himself")[2] a voice that speaks directly to him ("You are . . .").

The redactor of the Gospel of Matthew (Matt 3:16-17) retains the visionary perspective, but changes the personal address into a kind of third-person proclamation ("This is . . ."). He also adds that the *pneuma* is the "Spirit *of God*" and underscores the imagistic quality of the event with *hōsei* [the difference between this and Mark's *hōs* is obscured when the NRSV translates both words as "like"—Tr.], and has the dove *alighting on* Jesus.

The evangelist Luke reports these things (Luke 3:21-22) as if they were a real event *(egeneto),* not a vision: the Holy Spirit descends on Jesus "in bodily form" *(sōmatikō eidei)* like a dove. The voice from heaven is a personal address, as in Mark. However, the manuscript tradition also contains the quotation from Ps 2:7, "You are my Son, today I have begotten you," an Egyptian notion of the begetting of the Pharaoh by the god that was applied to the kingship in the First Testament.[3]

Finally, in the Fourth Gospel the whole event becomes a revelation given to the Baptizer, to which he gives testimony: the Spirit descended from heaven like a dove and rested on Jesus, and God revealed to him that this is the one who will baptize with Holy Spirit.

However, all the redactional accents—and we will return to some of them—remarkably enough do not touch the central image of the Spirit as a dove. The symbol appears, for whatever reasons, to have had a great degree of stability. What is it about this dove, which has remained a symbol of the Holy Spirit even to the present day in our churches? What significance does the Spirit acquire from the image of a bird? What kind of associations did the dove symbol awaken among the hearers (female *and* male) at the time when these texts were written? We cannot simply assume that the primary connotations of the dove for us, such as "peace," and "lovey-dovey," are nearly two thousand years old.

Even the newer gospel commentaries offer a disappointing paucity of material on these pericopes, very little that could help us to make a truly exact determination of the significance of the dove symbol in context. As a representative recent example let me refer to Joachim Gnilka's commentary on Mark.[4] Apparently Gnilka has no real idea what to do with the Spirit in the form of a dove. Like most exegetes he refers to Noah's dove in Gen 8:9, to the rabbinic theologians who illustrate the sweeping of the *rwḥ* over the waters (Gen 1:2) with the flight of a dove, and to the dove as the symbol of Israel. But this sweeping together of doves in the First Testament and Jewish tradition does not yield the *tertium comparationis* for our question about the equation Spirit = dove. It is not surprising that then Gnilka, and before him Leander Keck,[5] seek to solve the problem of the giver of meaning (the dove) by changing the recipient of the meaning. Thus Gnilka draws this conclusion: "The reality of the coming of the Spirit is described through a comparison with a dove. The Spirit does not have the form of a dove; the reference is to the fact that the whole event has a figurative character."[6] But such an interpretation is contrary to the text in every respect, because the recipient of the meaning is in any case the Spirit, and not its descent.

2. The Bird Messenger of the Ancient Near Eastern Love Goddesses

The route out of this dead end has been graded, in fact, not by Second Testament exegesis, but by Ancient Near Eastern and Greek iconography. Friedrich Sühling in his study of the dove as a religious symbol in Christian antiquity, which appeared in 1930,[7] presents a number of indications that in ancient pagan conceptions the bird was, as such, sacred to the gods and was regarded as a form of appearance of the divine: "This view was a generalized cultural belief and Christians were also aware of it."[8] He specifies this general observation with reference to the dove as sacred to Astarte, Aphrodite, and in fact all the great love goddesses: "The dove possesses a special affinity to love. Probably for that reason it was the sacred bird of the love goddesses in antiquity."[9] In this connection Sühling also mentions the dove on the *sēmēion* in the temple at Hierapolis, the special role of the dove in the love poetry of the Roman authors, but also in the Song of Songs, and the idea of the dove as God's favorite bird in 2 Esd 5:26.[10]

Erwin R. Goodenough also, in the eighth volume of his encyclopedia of Jewish symbols in the Greco-Roman period (1958),[11] arrived, through his research into the dove symbol in Jewish art, at results that draw our attention to Ancient Near Eastern and Greco-Roman iconography. Antiquity recognized three elements of the dove symbol: the dove as figure and associative symbol or "familiar" of the female divinities, the dove as figure of the human soul, and (in Judaism) the dove as symbol of Israel. However, Judaism did not recognize the dove as symbol of the spirit. For the dove as associative symbolic bird of the pagan goddesses Goodenough relies largely on material that was collected by Kurt Galling for a short article on the dove in the second edition of the *RGG*.[12] Galling mentions the tiny clay houses with dove carvings from the temple of Ishtar in Assyria (3000 B.C.E.), from Bethshean (1500 B.C.E.), and from Cyprus (700 B.C.E.), as well as the dove as symbol of Atargatis, Derketo of Ashkelon, and Punic Tanith, the hierodules of the temple of Ishtar, called "doves," and isolated examples of doves as attributes of male divinities (Malatya). However, neither Galling nor Sühling establishes a connection between the content of the symbol of the dove as companion bird for the goddesses and baptism with the Spirit in the Second Testament.

In her doctoral dissertation of 1926, S. Hirsch in fact explicitly rejects such a connection.[13] Goodenough derives the Christian dove- as-Spirit from Hellenistic Judaism (Philo).[14] Hugo Gressmann tried to show, using Ancient Near Eastern iconographic material, that in Mark 1:10-11 *parr.* the election and crowning of Jesus by the dove (as a royal bird) symbolized the Ancient Near Eastern goddess. What is lacking in Gressmann's proof, however, and he himself had to admit this, is an important stage, namely any reference to the idea that the goddess caused a dove to descend on the head of the chosen ruler.[15]

Jan-Adolf Bühner then again attempted to establish a sense-connection on the basis of Goodenough's studies, in his article on "περιστερά," in *EDNT,* where he applies the idea of the "familiar" of the goddesses to baptism with the Spirit; "The dove thus appears as a familiar of the God of Israel. The Spirit in the form of a dove exhibits the union of Father and Son, which the heavenly voice speaks, as a charismatic-visionary reality."[16] Unfortunately, Bühner does not give a more precise description of the unity of Father and Son, which both in words and in parallel symbol has become the theme of the baptismal pericope. However, in my opinion the interpretation of the Holy Spirit as the "familiar" does not say enough about the biblical-theological sense of the symbol. How did, of all things, the dove move from association with the Ancient Near Eastern love goddesses and enter into such a central Second Testament tradition?

It appears that Bühner overlooked an important short study of the theme of the dove, which appeared in 1977 under the title *Vögel als Boten.*[17] Independent of the older works already mentioned, in this book Othmar Keel and Urs Winter collected representations of doves and other birds in the art of the Ancient Near East to aid in a new interpretation of Ps 68:12-14 and the title of

Psalm 56. An occasion for further engagement with the dove was its appearance in the metaphor of the eyes of the beloved, which are (like) doves (Song 1:15; 5:12). Keel explores this more thoroughly in a study on the metaphors of the Song of Songs.[18] In what follows I would like to summarize the results of both these studies, because they give us the crucial key to a precise understanding of the Spirit symbolism in Mark 1:10-11 *parr.*

In the second and first millennia B.C.E. the dove was the attribute animal *par excellence* of the Near Eastern love goddesses. The impressions of ancient Syrian cylinder seals (ca. 1750 B.C.E.) repeatedly show naked or disrobing goddesses from whom doves are flying away or flying from the goddess to her divine or royal partner.[19] Very similar depictions are also found on objects from the Late Bronze Period in Cyprus and northern Syria, and even in Neo-Assyrian glyptics.[20] Not always, but in many cases, such scenes are characterized by an almost naked eroticism, for example when the goddess offers herself seductively to her partner or when the carving depicts an intimate "banquet" or tête-a-tête.[21] That in this atmosphere the dove also connotes "erotic love" or acts as its messenger is obvious. These connotations are not absent even in less "libertine" illustrations and in other iconographic constellations.

As the attribute animal of Ishtar, for example, a single giant white dove marks her temple in a well-known wall painting from Mari (18th c. B.C.E.).[22] As early as the third millennium B.C.E.[23] and into the Roman period there are many instances in which temples are depicted on various kinds of painted and carved objects, and other instances of temple models adorned with doves. In the majority of cases these are temples of goddesses of Near Eastern origin: Ishtar, Anat, Astarte, Aphrodite.[24] Ancient Babylonian clay reliefs already depict goddesses with doves on their shoulders or on their thrones.[25] Molds and terra-cotta reliefs from Anatolia and Syria portray the naked goddess in a mandorla, flanked by doves.[26] A small bronze figure from Syria shows a goddess with a dove on her head, its wings outspread.[27] That the motif was not unknown in Israel is demonstrated by a finding from Hazor—an ivory spoon shaped as a woman's head flanked to left and right by doves (first half of the 8th c. B.C.E.)—and by a clay dove found together with so-called pillar goddesses in a grave in Lachish (700 B.C.E.).[28]

Beginning about the middle of the second millennium B.C.E. we find the dove goddess in Crete, Cyprus, and Mycene, and under Greek influence her cult enjoyed renewed popularity in the first millennium B.C.E.[29] In the Hellenistic period figurines of doves billing and cooing were popular offerings at the shrines of Aphrodite,[30] and the Roman Venus is also repeatedly found with a feathered companion, as we know from, among others, Virgil's *Aeneid* (6.193).[31] Greek coins from the Roman period (first century C.E.) show the goddess of the city of Ashkelon (Astarte/ Damaris) with a dove, and the dove goddess is also found on Cyprus, on coins of Caracalla (211–217).[32]

In ancient art the dove, as representative symbol or companion animal, signals the presence and sphere of the goddess. The billing and cooing of these birds, interpreted by ancient authors as a loving kiss, would have been an important reason why the dove in particular was associated with the love goddess.[33] The color of the dove can very seldom be determined from the objects bearing it (cf. the wall painting at Mari), but apparently there was an old tradition that doves, especially those of the Palestinian-Syrian goddess, were white,[34] which means they were a specially-bred form of the cliff dove (*columbiu liviu,* Hebrew יונה, *jonah,* Greek *peristera*).[35]

In many cases the dove does not simply fly around the goddess, but assumes message-bearing functions. It flies to the goddess's partner with a message of love and tenderness. The fact that the same message can also be sent by a ruler/god to a female partner is shown by a drinking scene on an ancient Syrian cylinder seal in Krakow.[36] On another piece we find the dove before an enthroned, probably male divinity who is being worshipfully greeted by a man and a woman.[37]

Othmar Keel offers proof from Egyptian iconography that doves were to be understood as *messengers* of love: there is evidence from Egypt as late as the Ptolemaic period of a custom of loosing beautifully decorated birds at victory and enthronement celebrations as emblems of triumph and of the enthronement of the godking; from there it exercised influence on Palestine and Syria as well.[38] In those places, however, it seems that the ducks and blue rollers typical of Egypt have been replaced by doves,[39] as illustrated, for example, in a very beautiful ivory carving from Megiddo

(1350–1150 B.C.E.) where the victorious return of a Canaanite city ruler is celebrated by, among other things, flying doves.[40] In this symbolic function as bird-messengers, the bringers of good news (which, incidentally, has little in common with our use of homing pigeons),[41] doves appear in the First Testament in the Flood story and in Pss 56 (title: MT 56:1) and 68:13 (MT 68:14).[42] The stereo-typical comparison of the eyes of the beloved with doves in the Song of Songs means, when we include both connotations, "love-goddess/love" and "bird-messenger/messenger of joy," "your glances are happy messages of love; they proclaim your love. They invite love."[43] That this is a complete, and therefore also—indeed especially—an erotic-physical love is clear not only from the tradition of the dove-symbol described above but also from the context and character of the Song of Songs, which is a collection of secular love songs.[44]

3. A Divine Turtledove in the Second Testament

In his study on the metaphors in the Song of Songs, Othmar Keel has already pointed out that both of the Ancient Near Eastern/Second Testament associations of the dove symbol we have mentioned are presumed in Mark 1:10-11 as familiar to the readers: here the Spirit, as a dove, like the doves of the love goddess, communicates the love of God to this man Jesus. The words that are addressed to Jesus from heaven say the same thing: they are a message, and the message is about the love of God.[45]

Eugen Ruckstuhl was the first Second Testament exegete to un-hesitatingly accept Othmar Keel's suggestion, in his contribution to a Festschrift for Eduard Schweizer.[46] Let us be clear: what the research of Urs Winter and Othmar Keel has gained for us is the messenger connotation[47] and a crucial accentuation of the love symbolism as erotic symbolism. Erwin R. Goodenough had al-ready quite correctly and persistently insisted on this accent[48] against Friedrich Sühling, who wanted to refashion the Ancient Near Eastern dove symbol in Christian contexts *a priori* into a symbol of *dilectio* or *caritas*.[49]

Precisely here we reach an initial focal point of our investiga-tion. When the Second Testament adopts the dove symbol it most certainly adopts its erotic-emotional associations as well. As late as the third century C.E. the pagan dove goddess was known in Palestine (Ashkelon) and Gentile Christian groups would have found the imagery in the story of Jesus' baptism immediately familiar against that background. What the dove retains, even though in the baptism story it does not come flying from an Ancient Near Eastern goddess, is the element of erotic love.[50] It is the symbol of the Spirit of love, which is all-encompassing and not spiritualized. The love of God for her/his beloved is anything but purely spiritual and platonic; it is more than *dilectio* and *caritas:* God loves with tenderness, passion, and impetuous enthusiasm—that, after all, is the joyful news of the dove for Jesus, and at the same time its wooing invitation to return this sensual divine love.

Unfortunately there is no sense of the eroticism of the Holy Spirit in Christian churches today. In none of the pertinent theological lexicons is there the faintest indication of anything in this direction to be found under the word "(Holy) Spirit," and in our churches the dove of the Spirit is understood more as the dove of (divine) peace than as a divine turtledove. The holy and the erotic are diligently kept apart in our times, whereas the Ancient Near East never separated them· eroticism and sexuality enter into the closest possible connection with the very pictorial ideas of the sphere of the gods and goddesses,[51] and the dove, as we have seen, had its place in the temple, that is, in the earthly place associated with the presence of the divine.[52] This inseparability of *eros* and the sacred was also familiar to ancient Israel, for (to take a few examples) the lotus, the pomegranate, and the palmetto had an important place in the interior decoration of Solomon's Temple (1 Kings 7:17-20, 26, 42). We also find all these symbols of life and fertility in the love poems of the Song of Songs (Song 2:1, 16; 4:3, 5, 13; 7:8-9) in erotic contexts.[53]

Two major sets of questions remain to be explored in connection with this attempt to shed light on a Second Testament text with the aid of Ancient Near Eastern iconography:

1. Neither the Second nor the First Testament has found erotic language for God (or the Spirit). In the First Testament God is undoubtedly a male and a "bachelor"; while *rwḥ,* "the storm/spirit," is grammatically feminine, she is "scarcely, if at all, an independently

acting female entity."[54] In the Second Testament God is primarily the "Father in heaven," and this image of God also dispenses with all sexual-erotic components. In such an *eros*-hating context, how did the dove symbol gain access to such an important pericope in the Second Testament? We will have to look for the mediating factors between the pagan symbolism and the theology of the primitive Christian movement/communities, since it is rather improbable that that communication could have happened *solely* through knowledge of the cult of some Palestinian city goddesses.

2. We need to attempt to understand what were the circumstances in the early Church that caused the dove to lose the connotations relating it to the female love divinities, so that today it finds its place in our churches as a symbol of the (male) Holy Spirit without creating any reaction. Do the so-called Apocrypha and Pseudepigrapha, or the writings of the Fathers of the Church, give us any indications about the fate of the dove in the first three centuries?

4. The Dove as Symbol of Wisdom in Philo of Alexandria

Regarding the bridge between the pagan symbol and the early Christian theology/pneumatology or christology, we may follow a very valuable indication from Erwin R. Goodenough, who connects the dove as symbol of the Holy Spirit at the Jordan with some remarks of Philo of Alexandria.[55] In *Quis rerum Divinarum Heres* (126–128) Philo reports that *theia sophia,* divine Wisdom, is also called "turtledove" *(trygōn),* and that human wisdom, *anthrōpinē sophia,* is called "rock dove" *(peristera):*

> Divine Wisdom is a hermitess,
> for, because of the one God
> whose possession she is
> she loves to be alone—
> symbolically she is called turtledove—
> mild, gentle, and fond of society is the other
> who likes to abide in the cities of humanity
> and is fond of the society of mortals;
> this one is compared to the rock dove (127–28).

Goodenough presupposes that Philo is here referring to a Hellenistic-Jewish tradition according to which personified Wisdom—the one who is with God and the other who goes about among human beings—is compared to two kinds of doves. In the same book (at 230–243) the doves then become symbols of the "archetypical Logos above us."[56] For Philo, in addition, Sophia, who has a central soteriological function, in her function as revealer is identical with the *pneuma*.[57]

Does the key to the tradition history of the dove in the Second Testament lie in Hellenistic-Jewish or Gnostic Wisdom speculation? It is problematic, of course, to discover what group's teaching Philo may here be referring to. Scholars have often emphasized the eclecticism of his writings: "We find in his work numerous elements from the tradition of Greek philosophy . . . as well as . . . influences from Near Eastern and Hellenistic mysteries, quite apart from the tradition of Jewish theology, whose representative Philo feels himself to be."[58]

Since within the scope of this short chapter we cannot possibly enter into complex discussions about the dependency, influences, and cross-connections between Jewish, Hellenistic, Gnostic, and Christian Wisdom speculation, in what follows the results of the comprehensive research of Elisabeth Schüssler Fiorenza on the one hand, and a brief study by James M. Robinson on the other, will serve as the primary bases for our investigation.

Because the hypostasizing of Wisdom, *ḥkmh,* whom we also encounter in the First Testament in Proverbs, Job, and Wisdom, was experienced as a foreign body in Jewish theology, and because the similarity between Jewish and Gnostic texts cannot be accidental, for a long time people attempted to discover the myth of a foreign goddess, or to reconstruct a Wisdom myth that might have served as a religious-historical parallel and background for all these texts. Ulrich Wilckens also still suspected that the basis for the attractive power of Jewish and Gnostic Wisdom speculation in the Hellenistic period lay in the fact "that the personal figure of Wisdom in Judaism and Gnostic Sophia originally had the same religious-historical background."[59] However, no one ever got very far beyond this point because no individual myth or single goddess could be singled out as the one discernible behind the figure of Wisdom in the Jewish writings. Ishtar, Aphrodite, Psyche, Demeter, and Kore, but especially Maat and Isis, were discussed as religious-historical godmothers of "Wisdom," but a clear choice proved to be impossible.[60]

Here Elisabeth Schüssler Fiorenza emphasizes the urgent need to make a distinction between mythical material and reflective mythology:

> Reflective mythology is not a living myth but is rather a form of theology appropriating mythical language, material, and patterns from different myths, and it uses these patterns, motifs, and configurations for its own theological concerns. Such a theology is not interested in reproducing the myth itself or the mythic material as they stand, but rather taking up and adapting the various mythical elements to its own theological goal and theoretical concerns.[61]

The methodological distinction is helpful for exegesis of all the Wisdom literature, Philo, the Gnostic writings, and the Second Testament christological hymns. The thesis that the hypostasis of Wisdom did not arise, in religious-historical terms, from a goddess myth, but instead arrived by way of reflective mythologizing at a similarity with a large number of ancient goddesses is confirmed by the studies of Othmar Keel and Urs Winter.

An influence of Egyptian Maat on the figure of Wisdom has been postulated repeatedly during the last twenty years.[62] Now Othmar Keel has used iconography to demonstrate the Egyptian background of Wisdom, who plays before God during the creation of the world, in a little book on playful Wisdom in Prov 8:30-31. Personified Wisdom, as presented in Proverbs 8, combines features of Egyptian Hathor, Maat, and the "joking divine consort."[63] However, Keel avoids asserting direct historical dependence.

Urs Winter, in his recent book *Frau und Göttin,* follows Keel in this reticence. In addition to what Keel has demonstrated, Winter has been able, by use of the iconography of the Syrian-Canaanite goddess, especially Syrian glyptics, to show the probability of a Canaanite mediation between Egyptian Maat and the Jewish hypostasis of Wisdom. Especially important is the erotic element, which is lacking in Egyptian Maat in contrast to playful Wisdom:[64] "The eroticizing and playful aspect of the goddess cannot be demonstrated iconographically anywhere as well as in Syrian glyptics, and I would therefore not exclude the possibility that it is not Maat, but the disrobing Syrian-Canaanite goddess who represents the 'prototype' of the *mśḥqt* of personified Wisdom."[65]

The shifting variety of mythical elements, as we can see again here, once more leads us back to the realm of the Ancient Near Eastern goddesses and their erotic aura. We will not go wrong in supposing that Philo is citing a "reflective mythology" that has endowed personified Wisdom with the mythical element of the goddesses' dove. We will now show that earliest Christianity thought and spoke of Jesus, God, and the Spirit in Wisdom categories, and that it is precisely that Wisdom christology/theology/pneumatology that explains the migration of the dove into Mark 1:10-11 *parr.* and reveals its deeper theological dimensions.

5. Jesus-Sophia and God-Sophia in Early Christianity

In Jewish-Hellenistic Wisdom speculation, Wisdom is represented as a heavenly figure.[66] She is preexistent, participates in creating, lives in close union with God, and seeks an abode among human beings. Especially amazing is the variety of sexual images associated with Wisdom: she is mother, wife, lover,[67] beloved, virgin, and bride (cf. Job 28; Proverbs 1–9; Sir 24:1-2; Wis 7:21-26). Sometimes it is said that she is now hidden and unapproachable (Job 28:13; Sir 1:20-32); in other texts (Wis 7:24-27; Sir 1:10, 15; 6:20-22) she can be found by those who seek her and who are among the elect. Yet again it is said (Sir 24:7-17; Bar 3:9; 4:2 LXX) that Wisdom has found her resting place *(anapausis)* in Israel and Jerusalem. Sophia comes to her chosen and thus speaks through the First Testament prophets (Wis 7:27; 10:16).

In the Wisdom theology of the Q-community John the Baptizer and Jesus together formed the high point of this salvation history involving the emissaries of Sophia that began in the First Testament (Luke 7:33-35 *par.* Matt 11:18-19).[68] Jesus and John are Sophia's outstanding children, and Jesus' primacy over John is only formulated in terms of the Son of Man tradition. James M. Robinson emphasizes, however, that the latest Q stratum no longer understands Jesus only as spokesman for Wisdom, but speaks of him as Sophia herself. The exclusive mutual knowledge of Father and Son as formulated in Luke 10:21-22 *par.* Matt 11:25-27 must also be understood as a Wisdom concept. Here, as in the later stages of the Jewish Wisdom tradition, the Son has the same function as heavenly Sophia, speaking as the sole revealer and savior. Only the Father knows the Son, as in the Wisdom tradition only God knows Wisdom, who is otherwise hidden. Only when she reveals herself is she recognized. Like heavenly Sophia, the Son is the sole mediator of divine revelation, and the content of that heavenly revealed knowledge is Wisdom or the Son her/himself.[69]

This last stage of Q thus already reveals the Sophia christology that will then be developed by Matthew (cf. especially 11:28-30). The exclusive nature of Sophia is assigned to the Son, who is identified with Jesus. In the first half of the second century C.E. the identification of Jesus with Sophia, or the idea that Wisdom found her resting place in Jesus, was widespread. We find it in the Gospel of Thomas and the Gospel of the Hebrews, as well as in Justin Martyr's writings.[70] Especially interesting for us is a quotation Jerome chose (in his commentary on Isa 11:2) from the Gospel of the Hebrews. It reads:

> And it came to pass when the Lord was come up out of the water, the whole fount of the Holy Spirit descended upon him and rested on him and said to him: My Son, in all the prophets was I waiting for thee that thou shouldest come and I might rest in thee. For thou art my rest; thou art my first-begotten Son that reignest for ever.[71]

The editors of the text point out the relationship of this text to Wisdom (Sir 24:7; Wis 7:27),[72] and Robinson writes: "The standard Sophia *topos* is unmistakable, even though the passage, describing Jesus' baptism, uses the equivalent term Spirit, since this is the term the tradition used for what came on Jesus at baptism."[73]

It is true that we cannot posit *a priori* that this Sophia-christological version of the baptismal account from the Gospel of the Hebrews can be read into Mark 1:10-11, but I would like to propose the thesis that the Second Testament baptismal account in all four gospels was not only peripherally influenced by a Wisdom "mythologoumenon," but that it was conceived in terms of Wisdom *theology*—already beforehand, in the *Vorlagen* or sources of Mark and John—and that it was handed on by the redactors of the gospels with that understanding.

The baptismal event reveals that Jesus is the person in whom/ upon whom Wisdom/Spirit finds rest. The voice from heaven is the voice of divine Sophia/Sophia-God, who has found her/his Chosen One. As symbol of Sophia, as message of her love, and as sign of her presence in Jesus, the dove of the "goddess" Sophia/ the *pneuma* descends upon him.

In the Gospel of John the dove becomes a sign for the Baptizer that Jesus is the Christ he has announced. The accompanying revelation in words tells him that this is the one who will baptize with Holy Spirit. Since the context of the Prologue on the preexistent Logos (the only Son of the Father) in the Fourth Gospel reveals great affinity to Wisdom conceptions, in the Johannine community the dove would have been understood as the symbol of Wisdom, the Spirit, or the Logos.[74]

In Mark the message of the voice is a free quotation from a proclamation about the Servant of God in Deutero-Isaiah (Isa 42:1):

> Here is my servant, whom I uphold,
> my chosen, in whom my soul delights;
> I have put my spirit upon him;
> he will bring forth justice to the nations.

Through the heavenly message the Wisdom-symbolic event is closely linked with the fulfillment of a First Testament promise in the light of which Jesus appears as Servant of God, Chosen One, New Moses (cf. Mark 9:7; Deut 18:15), and Son, on whom the Spirit of God rests. Luke's and Matthew's correction of Mark's *eis auton* was probably done for the purpose of quoting the First Testament (LXX) more accurately. In all the gospels, then, the baptismal account transmits a Sophia theology in which Jesus is understood as prophet and emissary of Wisdom, but also already as the incarnation of Sophia, as that Wisdom who is in the most intimate possible relationship with God.[75]

In the context of Matthew's gospel the further development by which Jesus is identified with (preexistent) Sophia by way of the theme of the Servant of God is already visible.[76] In Matt 12:18-21 the fulfillment citation from Isa 42:1-4 becomes an interpretive text for Jesus' saving actions: God's "beloved" (!) is infinitely gentle ("he will not break a bruised reed"), like God-Sophia him/herself. To the Baptizer's question whether Jesus is the one who is to come, Jesus responds with a quotation of Isa 42:7 (cf. 35:5; 61:1). According to Matt 11:2, 19 Wisdom is justified by Jesus' powerful *deeds* and, despite these deeds, which in the First Testament the Servant of God does at the command of God and as God's mediator, Jesus, as Servant of God/Sophia, will be rejected (Matt 11:20-24). The climax of this identification of Jesus with Sophia in Matthew's gospel is found in 11:28.

If this interpretation is correct we have in Mark 1:10-11 *parr.* a very important witness to the fact that the evangelists knew and adopted a tradition[77] in which Jesus was understood to be the emissary of Sophia or even the incarnation of Sophia. In the earliest Jesus tradition Sophia christology is closely connected to a Sophia theology that conceived God in female form as divine Sophia.[78] God's limitless kindness is divine Sophia, whose yoke is light, who will open a future for the poor and heavy-laden, the rejected and the oppressed, and who demands no sacrifices. But the kindness and friendliness (of the emissary) of Sophia are rejected (cf. Luke 11:49), and her prophets must die (Luke 13:34). The three synoptic gospels know the saying about the impossibility of forgiveness for blasphemy against the Spirit (Mark 3:28-29 *parr.*):

> "Truly I tell you, people will be forgiven for their sins and whatever blasphemies they utter; but whoever blasphemes against the Holy Spirit can never have forgiveness, but is guilty of an eternal sin."

Here is another logion in which Jesus is unmistakably depicted as "God's kindness" in person, divine Sophia, whom no human person dare reject. Those who reject Jesus reject God, reject Sophia.[79] Here Wisdom is again referred to as (Holy) Spirit.

As Elisabeth Schüssler Fiorenza has shown, this exchange of concepts was also known to the Christian missionary movement:

The risen Lord was identified not only with the Spirit of God, but also with the Sophia of God (cf. 1 Cor 1:24-30); it appears that the pre-Pauline Christian missionary movement even adopted a Sophia christology as normative (cf. Phil 2:6-11; 1 Tim 3:16; Col 1:15-20; Eph 2:14-16; Heb 1:3; 1 Pet 3:18, 22). Paul confronts it in 1 Corinthians 1; it is possible that it was developed and preached by Apollos.[80]

As we have seen above, the joining of the First Testament theologoumenon that God puts the divine Spirit on prophets and the elect, or in Deutero-Isaiah on the Servant of God, with the Wisdom idea that God sends Wisdom to the elect and that Wisdom comes to human beings through prophets and sages builds the bridge that is needed here. Thus in the book of Wisdom (9:17) we already find a well-developed synonymous equation of Wisdom and Holy Spirit:

> Who has learned your counsel,
> unless you have given wisdom
> and sent your holy spirit from on high?

The motif of sending from on high has unmistakably entered into the shaping of our Second Testament pericope.

The exchange of the two concepts was made possible, for one thing, by their grammatically feminine gender in Hebrew and Arabic.[81] In addition, Jewish-Hellenistic Wisdom speculation, but especially Philo, had prepared the way for the theological connection of Sophia and Pneuma, and even Sophia and Logos (cf. John 1:1-14).[82]

Since both Apollos and Philo were Alexandrian theologians well versed in Scripture, we may suppose that this Wisdom pneumatology (and the mythologoumenon of the dove it contained) originated in that location, one of the bases for the early spread of Christianity.[83] God, Jesus, and the Pneuma were mythologized as personified Wisdom. Elisabeth Schüssler Fiorenza attributes the spread of mythological ideas like this, or more precisely the necessity of understanding them through the use of reflective mythology, especially to the Isis cult, which experienced a major renaissance and spread widely in the Hellenistic-Roman period and, as she is able to show, had an important theological and group-sociological influence on Christian communities in the earliest period.[84]

6. The Early Church's Interpretations of the Dove at the Jordan

The minimal differences in the application of the Sophia imagery to the three divine persons are explained by the fact that we cannot presume the development of a trinitarian theology in the Second Testament and early Christian writings before the fourth century. It was only the Council of Constantinople that established fundamental principles, for example, regarding the Spirit as person.[85]

A glance at the early Church witnesses that give information about the interpretation of the dove at the Jordan shows that they reflect just this situation as far as the Trinity is concerned. Friedrich Sühling[86] collected a whole series of examples from the second and third centuries, all of which show that the early Fathers (Justin, Clement of Alexandria, Tertullian [?], Lactantius, Jerome) and the Christian poets saw the dove not as a symbol of the Spirit, but as a symbol of the Logos, the heavenly Christ, who descended on Jesus. From this conception developed, among other things, the tradition of the dove in the Annunciation scene, according to which it is to be interpreted as the Logos, which flies into Mary's body and takes on flesh. This motif had an enduring influence on Christian art.[87]

Origen, in his homily on the Song of Songs, calls the turtledove *(turturis)* and the (house) dove *(columba)* figures of the Holy Spirit (and the bird at the baptism was a *columba!*).[88] Cyril of Alexandria was still familiar with both the turtledove *(trygōn)* and the rock dove *(peristera)* as symbols of Christ.[89] However, it appears from these witnesses that knowledge of the origins of the dove symbol had already been lost. (Cyril, for example, speaks of the eloquence and gentleness of these birds to explain why they are images of Christ.) Nothing is left of the association of the dove with female divinities or its (erotic) love symbolism.

We also find the dove at the Jordan as an image both of the heavenly Christ and of the Pneuma and Logos or Jesus in early

Church witnesses from the second and third centuries that reveal influences from Christian Gnosticism.[90] In the so-called Gospel of the Ebionites, from the first half of the second century, which contains a baptismal account that harmonizes the synoptic versions, the dove is the symbol of the Holy Spirit who enters into Jesus.[91] The sixth book of the Christian Sibylline Oracles, which may have been composed in the second to third centuries,[92] begins with a reminiscence of the baptismal event:

> 6.6 Who first, escaping from fire, shall see God
> 7 Coming in sweet spirit, on the white wings of a dove.

Other manuscripts, instead of *pneuma hēdy,* have *theon opsetai hēdyn,* "the sweet God."[93] In the seventh book the *peleia* appears again as Spirit-dove (v. 67) and as Logos-dove (vv. 77-84).[94] Recalling the baptism in fire, one should release a dove while praying, pour water into the fire, and cry out:

> 7.82 "As the Father begot thee as Logos, I send forth the bird,
> Swift messenger of words, as Logos, with holy water
> Sprinkling thy baptism, through which thou didst come out
> of fire."

In Odes of Solomon 24 (second century C.E.) we find her as the dove of Christ:

> 24.1 The dove flew over the head of our Lord Christ, for he was
> her head.
> 2 And she sang over him and her voice was heard.[95]

In *Pistis Sophia,* surviving in Coptic, the dove is the symbol of the Holy Spirit (ch. 141), the descending Christ (ch. 63), *and* God the Father (ch. 1).[96]

In contrast to all the witnesses above, the dove again appears in a female ambience in a eucharistic eulogy in the Gnostic Acts of Thomas, written in the third century in Syria. Among many primarily female titles, the "name" of Christ is offered hymnic praise (ch. 50):

Holy Dove
That bearest the twin young;
Come, hidden Mother.[97]

The context, and other passages in the Acts of Thomas (ch. 27),[98] indicate that this "holy dove" is to be understood as an image of the heavenly Sophia, who is entitled "mother," "mercy," "silence," and "truth," and who in Gnosticism is a kind of divine companion in the struggle of the earthly redeemer, the throne-companion of God, and the "name" that Jesus accepts at his baptism. In Bardesanian Gnosticism, with which the Acts of Thomas are here in contact, the "mother" is part of the heavenly pleroma.[99] In the Gospel of the Hebrews, a Jewish Christian writing probably originating in Egypt and also influenced by Gnosticism, Jesus says, according to Origen and Jerome, "Even so did my mother, the Holy Spirit, take me by one of my hairs and carry me away to the great mountain Tabor."[100]

We have a further interesting attestation of the fact that in Gnosticism the dove was interpreted as the Pneuma and the highest female divinity from Clement of Alexandria's *Excerpta ex Thodoto.* There Clement asserts that the Valentinians interpret the dove as *to pneuma tēs enthymēseōs tou patros,* and not as *to pneuma hagion* or *ton diakonon.* In the same document (7) the dove is identified with Gnosis as the highest female divinity.[101]

Hippolytus also cites the Gnostics Heracleon and Ptolemy: "(They) say that Jesus had a psychic body. That is why the Pneuma, that is, the Logos of the Mother from above, Sophia, descended as a dove at his baptism."[102]

Thus we have found a number of indications that the female connotations of the Pneuma and the dove symbolism survived longer in the Christian Gnostic environment than in the rest of early Christianity, where the (male) Logos conceptual schema appears to have eliminated all female elements very quickly. Although in Gnosticism the Pneuma, Logos, or Sophia had different individual functions within the theological world-structure than in Jewish-Hellenistic and Christian Wisdom speculation, all these personified female figures are similar in light of "reflective mythology," which was also proper already to Gnosticism.[103]

Hence the baptism in the Jordan could be interpreted without further ado as a mythologizing symbol and attribute in relation to the Gnostic Sophia-Mother figure.[104]

It is certain that the theological discourse of earliest Christianity about God, Jesus, and the Pneuma in Wisdom language and the reflective mythology associated with it was shoved into the background primarily because of the conflict with Gnosticism. Paul was struggling as early as 1 Corinthians with Gnostic Pneuma-Sophia doctrines (but does engage in a Wisdom pneumatology of his own!). He accuses the Corinthian groups of emptying the cross —a reproach that may have been directed at a typically Gnostic redeemer myth.[105] Because mythologizing Wisdom language received a special welcome in Gnostic circles—since it was already at home there—when Gnosticism was pushed aside as heresy the result was also a setting aside of the Wisdom-mythologizing female elements in early Christianity's image of Jesus and of God.

Solidifying this thesis would certainly require a more comprehensive treatment. Here, however, let us restrict ourselves to our Jordan dove. At the time of Irenaeus, as we can see from a section in his *Adversus haereses* (III.17.1), there was apparently a great need to identify boundaries in relation to (Gnostic) teachings that tried not to interpret the dove as the Holy Spirit (who for Irenaeus already had a very trinitarian identity):

> Obviously the apostles could have said that Christ descended on Jesus, or that the higher savior came on the Jesus of the economy, or the invisible one on the one from the demiurges—but since they knew no such thing, neither did they say it; if they had known it they would surely have said it. Instead what they did say is that the Spirit of God rested on him in the form of a dove. . . .[106]

There is a somewhat clearer reference to at least one of these doctrines (that of the Ophites) in *Adversus haereses* I.30.12-13, according to which at his baptism Sophia prepares Jesus as a vessel for her descending brother, Christ. Jesus is temporarily inhabited by Sophia and Christ, and both leave him before the crucifixion to return to the "imperishable eon."[107] The rejection of a Gnostic interpretation of the baptismal account, perhaps accompanied by misunderstanding of Wisdom-accented interpretations as Gnostic, or by intolerance of Logos-christological concepts—precise identifications can scarcely be derived from what Irenaeus has to say—thus was already beginning to extinguish the real symbolism of the dove and also to suppress Sophia christology. On the other hand, we still find in a "gnosticizing" Nag Hammadi document from the third to fourth centuries a clearly Wisdom-oriented christology:

> He is Wisdom.
> For he is Wisdom; he is also the Word [Logos].
> . . .
> It (Wisdom) is a holy kingdom . . .
> . . .
> The Wisdom of God became a type of fool for you
> so that it might take you up, O foolish one,
> and make you a wise man.
> And the Life died for you when he (Christ) was powerless, (15)
> so that through his death he might give life to you who have died.
> (*Teach. Silv.* 106.22b–107.16)[108]

Thus I see this investigation of dove symbolism as confirming the following sketch of christological developments, as described by Max Küchler in his studies on early Jewish Wisdom and its influence on the beginnings of Christianity:

> In terms of tradition history the old Wisdom christology is dying out in our New Testament texts. We can therefore probably assume that originally it played a much stronger role in the interpretation of Jesus. The "Jewish-Christian gnosticizing circles in Palestine" who presumably were "the agents of the oldest Sophia christology" were apparently driven by the anti-Gnostic front at a very early date into the heretical margins, and only found their voices again in Christian Gnosis. Hence it is understandable why the gnosticizing (e.g., *Silvanus*) and completely Gnostic writings there could be such a close joining of Sophia with Christ. The oldest Wisdom interpretational elements regarding Jesus must be located, in terms of time, even *before* Q, through whose selective collection some remnants have reached us. In tradition-historical terms, then, they are extremely close to the historical Jesus. . . .[109]

The fact that the Greek and Latin Fathers then remain faithful to the image of the dove at the Jordan for Christ and later the Holy Spirit[110] shows, on the one hand, the immense power of survival that images have, and on the other hand how their content can be reinterpreted. For in the Fathers the dove very quickly became a symbol of gentleness, innocence, purity, and even of (marital) chastity.[111] That symbolism also has demonstrable traditions leading back into antiquity, but it is certainly not on the scales when we are speaking of Mark 1:10-11 *parr.* When Augustine then later developed a pneumatology of the Spirit of love that would influence Western doctrinal traditions for a very long time, "love" was *caritas* and *dilectio.*[112] But it is no accident that in *De agone christiano* (XXII.24) Augustine expressly calls the love that the Spirit desired to show to humanity *amor spiritualis.*[113] In his emphasis on the spirituality of that love we may well detect a defense against a broader understanding of *amor* (as Venus!).

7. A Female Image of God in Christian Tradition

The reconstruction of the tradition-history of Mark 1:10-11 *parr.* has led us to the Ancient Near Eastern dove goddesses and the Wisdom theology of earliest Christianity. In that first period it was possible for Christians influenced by Jewish-Hellenistic Wisdom speculation and the renaissance of the Isis cult to speak of Jesus and God in the conceptual language of Sophia, who in her own person represented the generous kindness and love of God. The hypostasis of Wisdom was Christianity's great opportunity to integrate female and erotic elements into a monotheistic religion in which God was thought of as a male. The members of the Jesus movement and the early missionary movement succeeded in introducing the female image of God in the manner of "reflective mythology," already modeled for youthful Christianity, and probably they succeeded first of all because Jesus understood himself as the final emissary of Sophia, and expressed his unique relationship to God in Sophia imagery.[114] Sophia theology was the decisive factor that made it possible for the Christian movement to be a community of equals in which the promise of Gal 3:28 was already a reality. Elisabeth Schüssler Fiorenza, in her magnificent sketch of a history of early Christian women, has demonstrated the connections between that theology and the emancipatory praxis of the early Christian communities with a wealth of material.[115] Because the liberation of human beings from patriarchal structures is central to the message about the reign of God,[116] because God and Jesus are anything but patriarchs, because both are one with female Sophia, women in early Christianity could be the subjects of their own history as disciples of Jesus, witnesses to his resurrection, apostles and ministers within their communities, and community leaders.

There remains for us Christians today the hope-filled task of recalling these emancipatory impulses for ourselves and for the Church. Subversive work on a theology that in the meantime has become totally androcentric and the lived praxis of a Church of "equal" brothers and sisters will have to go hand in hand if they are to lead us into genuine Christian freedom. Christian feminists are constantly confronted with the dilemma of the male image of God. I think that the early Christians' method of "reflective mythology," which successfully achieved the union of a monotheistic-male tradition with the female image of God, including its erotic elements,[117] can show us a possible way out of the problem of an androcentric religion, so that in the future women will no longer be forced out of Christianity and the Church or leave in resignation because for them the traditional image of God symbolizes not freedom, but centuries of oppression of their female ancestors in faith. We women today can call on Jesus Sophia and God-Sophia as a very important, even though not dominant tradition, in order to change the image of God *within* Christianity and the Church, because, as Judy Chicago says, "our heritage is our power."[118]

NOTES

* This chapter on the symbolism of the dove in Mark 1:10-11 first appeared in 1986. Five years later it was adduced, among other things, as a reason why the official Church license to teach theology should be denied me. Some details on the controversy surrounding this article appeared in an extensive documentary collection in the periodical *Publik-Forum* in

1992. I am aware that the article has its weaknesses with regard to Gnostic writings and the Church Fathers. The tradition-historical reconstruction of the symbolism of the dove, which is traced from the Ancient Near Eastern witnesses through Wisdom symbolism and Philo of Alexandria, can be questioned, as can any historical reconstruction. But the question is whether anyone to that point (anyone at all) had offered a coherent interpretation of the dove in the Second Testament baptism pericopes. As far as I can see, that is not the case. Konrad Huber, in a recent article that offers little that is new, discusses the old positions and maintains the conclusion that the dove is used adverbially to give a more precise description of the descent of the Holy Spirit, so that the comparison is only formal, depicting the manner of flight. The major German-language gospel commentaries appearing since 1986 either offer no explanation of the dove at all, or withdraw to the by no means persuasive "adverbial" interpretation, which does nothing at all to explain why the text speaks of a dove and not more generally of a bird. That the administrators of a patriarchal Church hierarchy take offense at the erotic sensuousness of a symbol associated with the Holy Spirit is not terribly surprising. For centuries the Western tradition, unlike the Eastern, has repressed Wisdom and hence her former resemblance to a goddess from among the ideas pertaining to the triune God. Alterations in the image of God, especially reminiscences of God's femaleness, represented a threat to the male Church, because ultimately they undermined the primacy of men. Mary Daly pointedly expressed this mutual relationship, as regards Church and social relationships, years ago with the formula: "when God is a male, the male is God." It is almost embarrassing to see how notable churchmen make a theological slalom run when the female nature of God is the subject. In the sentence, "Wisdom is Israel's God in the image of a woman," the word "is" is suspected of making an ontological statement. The analogical statement "God is Father" has never been suspect, even though there are just as many reasons for suspicion. Theologically, both sentences are equally valid, not as ontological statements, but as statements about God using comparisons.

See Konrad Huber, " ΟΣ ΠΕΡΙΣΤΕΡΑ. Zu einem Motiv in den Tauferzählungen der Evangelien," *Protokolle zur Bibel* 4 (1995) 87–101. For women's history in early Christianity we now have the foundational work of Anne Jensen, *God's Self-Confident Daughters. Early Christianity and the Liberation of Women*. Translated by O. C. Dean, Jr. (Louisville: Westminster/John Knox, 1996).

1. On this see Herbert Braun, "Entscheidende Motive in den Berichten über die Taufe Jesu von Markus bis Justin," *ZThK* 50 (1953) 39–42.

He also includes the traditions in the Gospel of the Hebrews, Justin, and Ignatius in his overview.

2. See below on the meaning of *eis auton.*

3. Hugo Gressmann, "Die Sage von der Taufe Jesu und die vorderasiatische Taubengöttin," *Archiv für Religionswissenschaft* 20: 1–40, 323–359, 9.

4. For what follows see Joachim Gnilka, *Das Evangelium nach Markus.* EKK II/1 (Zürich: Benziger; Neukirchen-Vluyn: Neukirchener Verlag, 1978) 52.

5. Leander Keck, "The Spirit and the Dove," *NTS* 17 (1970/71) 41–76.

6. Gnilka, *Das Evangelium nach Markus* 52.

7. Friedrich Sühling, *Die Taube als religiöses Symbol im christlichen Altertum. Römische Quartalschrift für christliche Altertumskunde und für Kirchengeschichte,* Suppl. 24 (Freiburg: Herder, 1930). This study treats the dove symbolism as found in textual and pictorial witnesses from Christian antiquity, and still represents the most comprehensive work on this theme.

8. Ibid. 15.

9. Ibid. 182–83; cf. 172 n. 163, 128 n. 22, 264–65, 295.

10. Ibid. 16, 183.

11. For what follows see Erwin R. Goodenough, *Jewish Symbols in the Greco-Roman Period* (New York: Pantheon, 1953–68) 8:27–46.

12. Hermann Gunkel and Leopold Zscharnack, eds., *Die Religion in Geschichte und Gegenwart; Handwörterbuch für Theologie und Religionswissenschaft,* völlig neubearb. Aufl., in Verbindung mit Alfred Bertholet, Hermann Faber und Horst Stephan. 5 vols. (Tübingen: J.C.B. Mohr [Paul Siebeck], 1927–31) 5:999–1000; cited at length in Goodenough, *Jewish Symbols* 8:27–28.

13. S. Hirsch, *Die Vorstellung von einem weiblichen* πνεῦμα ἅγιον *im Neuen Testament und in der ältesten christlichen Literatur. Ein Beitrag zur Lehre vom Heiligen Geist.* Diss. Berlin, 1926, 48.

14. *Jewish Symbols* 44. See also below.

15. Cf. Gressmann, "Die Sage," especially 359. Nevertheless, the iconographic material Gressmann collected on the various dove-goddesses in antiquity is of value, independent of his thesis.

16. Jan-Adolf Bühner, "περιστερα," *EDNT* 3:184–86.

17. Othmar Keel, *Vögel als Boten: Studien zu Ps 68, 12-14, Gen 8, 6-12, Koh 10, 20 und dem Aussenden von Botenvögeln in Ägypten. Mit einem Beitr. von Urs Winter zu Ps 56,1 und zur Ikonographie der Göttin mit der Taube.* OBO 14 (Fribourg: Universitätsverlag; Göttingen: Vandenhoeck & Ruprecht, 1977).

18. Othmar Keel, *Deine Blicke sind Tauben. Zur Metaphorik des Hohen Liedes.* SBS 114/115 (Stuttgart: Katholisches Bibelwerk, 1984) 53–62.

19. Othmar Keel, *Vögel als Boten,* plates 15–19, 23; idem, *Deine Blicke,* plates 46–50; for the disrobing goddess cf. Urs Winter, *Frau und Göttin. Exegetische und ikonographische Studien zum weiblichen Gottesbild im Alten Israel und in dessen Umwelt.* OBO 53 (Fribourg: Universitätsverlag; Göttingen: Vandenhoeck & Ruprecht, 1983) 272–83.

20. Othmar Keel, *Deine Blicke* 61, and plates 51–52.

21. Such banquet scenes are always associated with lust for life in the Ancient Near East, and they involve drinking, music, and the pleasures of love. On this see Winter, *Frau und Göttin,* especially 253–60.

22. Keel, *Vögel als Boten,* plate 20; idem, *Deine Blicke,* plate 43.

23. See Kurt Galling's article in *RGG*[2] (n. 12 above).

24. Othmar Keel, *Deine Blicke,* especially 60, and plates 40–45.

25. Cf. Keel, *Vögel als Boten,* plates 10–12.

26. Ibid., plate 21 (Kültepe, ca. 1700 B.C.E.); plate 22 (Alalach, 1358–1285 B.C.E.).

27. Ibid., plates 27a–d (1800–1600 B.C.E.), in New York.

28. For the preceding cf. Keel, *Deine Blicke,* especially 62.

29. Cf. especially Keel, *Vögel als Boten* 74–75.

30. Keel, *Deine Blicke* 59, with n. 142 and plate 39.

31. For the dove in the work of Greek and Roman poets cf. Friedrich Sühling, *Die Taube* 182, and Keel, *Deine Blicke,* especially 59.

32. George Francis Hill, *Catalogue of the Greek Coins of Palestine (Galilee, Samaria, and Judaea)* (Bologna: A. Forni, 1965) 58, 104–40 (Ashkelon, with a great many examples from the period between the second century B.C.E. and the third century C.E.). The latest example of the dove goddess is from the time of Macrinus, 217/18 C.E. The oldest examples in George Francis Hill, *Catalogue of the Greek Coins of Cyprus* (Bologna: A. Forni, 1964) are three coins from Paphos showing Aphrodite, with the goddess on the front and a dove in profile on the reverse (Paphos, nos. 46–48). They derive from the period approximately from 400 to 330 B.C.E. Some coins from outside Cyprus, from Sardis and Pergamon, but also those from Paphos (Pl. 17,4-6) from the period of Septimius Severus and Caracalla (Imperial nos. 54, 59) show the shrine of the goddess with doves seated on each side.

33. On this see Keel, *Deine Blicke* 59. Another explanation is that at a very early time people heard doves as calling "Dumuzi," and so the bird became the companion of Inana/Ishtar, who calls after Dumuzi (cf. ibid. 59–60 n. 142a).

34. Cf. ibid. 56–57 for a citation of Charon (440 B.C.E.) in Athenaios of Neucratis (200 C.E.), according to whom the first white doves came to Greece in 492 B.C.E. Tibullus writes that white doves were sacred to the Palestinian Syrians and appeared in Palestine in great flocks. Bathing in milk (Song 5:12) also has associations with the white dove.

35. Cf. Othmar Keel, Max Küchler, and Christoph Uehlinger, *Orte und Landschaften der Bibel. Ein Handbuch und Studien-Reiseführer zum Heiligen Land I: Geographisch-geschichtliche Landeskunde.* OLB I (Zürich: Benziger; Göttingen: Vandenhoeck & Ruprecht, 1984) 137. We will return later to the turtledove (*streptopelia turtur,* Hebrew *tor,* Greek *trygōn*) with its two black and white spots on the side of the throat.

36. Keel, *Deine Blicke,* plate 49.

37. Keel, *Vögel als Boten,* plate 17.

38. Ibid.; see especially ch. 5, 103–42.

39. Similarly, in the Flood story in the First Testament the raven that is otherwise common in such stories is replaced by a dove (ibid., ch. 3). Here it seems obvious that the popularity of the dove in Syro-Palestinian iconography has left its mark.

40. Keel, *Vögel als Boten* 140 and plate 43. See other examples at pp. 139–40 and plate 42, the impression of a cylinder seal from Tel Adshul (1350–1100 B.C.E.)

41. On this see ibid. 91 n. 1, and Keel, *Deine Blicke* 58 n. 137.

42. The title for Psalm 56 is "The Dove of the Far-off Gods," and Urs Winter (in Keel, *Vögel als Boten* 36) suggests translating Ps 68:13 as: "Even though you (also) lie between saddlebags, the wings of the dove will (nevertheless) be covered with silver, and her pinions with green gold."

43. Keel, *Deine Blicke* 62.

44. For the origins and character of the Song of Songs see ibid. 12–13.

45. Keel, *Deine Blicke* 58. See also the reference in *Orte und Landschaften der Bibel* 1:139.

46. Eugen Ruckstuhl, "Jesu als Gottessohn im Spiegel des markinischen Taufberichtes," in Ulrich Luz and Hans Weder, eds., *Die Mitte des Neuen Testaments. Festschrift für E. Schweizer zum siebzigsten Geburtstag* (Göttingen: Vandenhoeck & Ruprecht, 1983) 193–220, at 200ff. and 213–14. Ruckstuhl cites (n. 27) still another older periodical article by Othmar Keel on Song of Songs 1:15; 4:1.

47. Interesting in this connection is a short note in Goodenough, *Jewish Symbols* 8:32. The observation that Aphrodite's chariot is sometimes drawn by doves leads him to suggest "that they bring her to men, or represent her power of motion."

48. *Jewish Symbols* 8:39. Goodenough rejects the idea "that all pagans thought of love only in physical terms, all Christians only in 'spiritual.'" As he shows, Plato and Plutarch already knew how to make subtle distinctions among the different forms of *amor* (ibid. 6–11).

49. Cf. Sühling, *Die Taube* 183.

50. Ditlef Nielsen, *Der dreieinige Gott in religionshistorischer Beleuchtung. I: Die drei göttlichen Personen* (Copenhagen: Gyldendalske Boghandel, Nordisk Forlag, 1922) 392–93 had already briefly explained the Spirit-dove at the baptism in the Jordan as a mythological reminiscence of the mother goddess of western Asia: "Everywhere among the north Semites and their neighboring peoples the dove was the holy bird and symbol of the mother goddess." It is true that the designation "mother goddess" is not accurate, but it is amazing to see what connections this historian of religions accepted (in what follows he also explores the mother-Spirit idea in Gnostic literature) and how he investigated the motherly-female element in the Trinity without any embarrassment—in 1922!

51. Cf., for example, the iconographic witnesses from Syria for the great significance of the "naked goddess" in Urs Winter, *Frau und Göttin,* ch. 2 passim, and ch. 3 c.

52. Ibid., especially 334–42 on sacred prostitution.

53. For the significance of the lotus (or lily) in the Song of Songs see Keel, *Deine Blicke* 63–77, and for the symbolism of the pomegranate in the Ancient Near East see the article by Jutta Börker-Klähn and Wolfgang Röllig in Erich Ebeling and Bruno Meissner, eds., *Reallexikon der Assyriologie* (Berlin and Leipzig: Walter de Gruyter, 1932–) 3:616–32.

54. "Only in 1 Kings 22:20-22 is *rwḥ* for one moment a lying spirit that brings destruction" (Urs Winter, *Frau und Göttin* 509 n. 167, with this thesis separates himself from numerous feminist studies of *rwḥ*). For a discussion of YHWH's *paredra* in the First Testament and the remnants of female qualities in this God and the systematic elimination of the goddess in Israel cf. ibid., especially 479–629.

55. Goodenough, *Jewish Symbols* 8:44–45.

56. Cf. ibid. 45.

57. Ulrich Wilckens, *Weisheit und Torheit. Eine exegetisch-religionsgeschichtliche Untersuchung zu 1 Kor 1 und 2.* Beiträge zur Historischen Theologie 26 (Tübingen: J.C.B. Mohr [Paul Siebeck], 1959) 145–59.

58. Ibid. 139.

59. Ibid. 195.

60. Elisabeth Schüssler Fiorenza, "Wisdom Mythology and the Christological Hymns of the New Testament," in Robert L. Wilken, ed., *Aspects*

of Wisdom in Judaism and Early Christianity (Notre Dame and London: University of Notre Dame Press, 1975) 28.

61. Ibid. 29.

62. See the survey by Urs Winter, *Frau und Göttin* 511–12, and especially the work of Christa Bauer-Kayatz, *Studien zu Proverbien 1–9. Eine form- und motivgeschichtliche Untersuchung unter Einbeziehung ägyptischen Vergleichsmaterials.* WMANT 22 (Neukirchen-Vluyn: Neukirchener Verlag, 1966).

63. Othmar Keel, *Die Weisheit spielt vor Gott. Ein ikonographischer Beitrag zur Deutung der m^{c}ṣaḥäqät in Sprüche 8,30f* (Fribourg: Universitätsverlag; Göttingen: Vandenhoeck & Ruprecht, 1974), especially 67.

64. The erotic component of *mśḥqt* in the description of personified Wisdom is an exception (cf. Winter, *Frau und Göttin* 528–29), which may be traced to the almost complete elimination of the (Canaanite) goddess from Israelite religion.

65. See ibid., especially 514–23. The idea of the exaltation of Wisdom and of Lady Wisdom as mediator also indicates convergences with the Syrian goddess as queen of heaven and intercessor/mediator in iconography (see ibid. 524–28).

66. For what follows see Elisabeth Schüssler Fiorenza, "Wisdom Mythology," 26–27; eadem, *In Memory of Her. A Feminist Theological Reconstruction of Christian Origins* (New York: Crossroad, 1983) 130–40.

67. Even in Qumran there was a psalm in deeply erotic language about the seeker of Wisdom who is in love and Wisdom the beloved, who find and love one another (cf. Max Küchler, *Frühjüdische Weisheitstraditionen. Zum Fortgang weisheitlichen Denkens im Bereich des frühjüdischen Jahweglaubens.* OBO 26 [Fribourg: Universitätsverlag; Göttingen: Vandenhoeck & Ruprecht, 1979] 102).

68. For this and what follows see James M. Robinson, "Jesus as Sophos and Sophia: Wisdom-Tradition and the Gospels," in *Aspects of Wisdom in Judaism and Early Christianity* (see n. 60 above) 1–16; Elisabeth Schüssler Fiorenza, *In Memory of Her* 132.

69. Cf. Siegfried Schulz, *Q: Die Spruchquelle der Evangelisten* (Zürich: Theologischer Verlag, 1972) 224–25; Robinson, "Jesus as Sophos and Sophia," 9–10.

70. Ibid. 12. In Justin (*Dial.* 100.4) we read that Jesus "was called Sophia . . . in the words of the prophets."

71. Translation in Wilhelm Schneemelcher, ed., *New Testament Apocrypha. I: Gospels and Related Writings.* Translated by Robert McLean Wilson (rev. ed. Louisville: Westminster/John Knox, 1991) 177.

72. Ibid. 174.

73. "Jesus as Sophos and Sophia," 12.

74. For Philo's theology as preparation for the interchangeability of Logos and Sophia in pre-Pauline Sophia christology and in the Prologue of John see Elisabeth Schüssler Fiorenza, *In Memory of Her* 191; cf. also Max Küchler, *Frühjüdische Weisheitstraditionen* 57–61.

75. Felix Christ also, in his study of the Sophia theology of the synoptics (*Jesus Sophia. Die Sophia-Christologie bei den Synoptikern.* AThANT 57 [Zürich: Zwingli, 1970], especially 153–54) concludes that Jesus was understood not only as "spokesman and bearer of Wisdom," but also as "Wisdom itself." Christ does not include the baptismal pericope in his study.

76. For what follows see Robinson, "Jesus as Sophos and Sophia," especially 10–11. For the joining of the Servant of God and Sophia see also Felix Christ, *Jesus Sophia* 70.

77. The relationship among Mark's *Vorlage,* John's sources, and possibly Q (see Robinson, "Jesus as Sophos and Sophia," 8), and the stages of development of Sophia theology they may have presented is a question that must remain open at present. However, Robinson's conclusions that Q already tended in a last stage to identification of Jesus with Sophia, and the results of Max Küchler's studies (*Frühjüdische Weisheitstraditionen,* especially 585) permit us to posit such a concept even in the first generation.

78. For the following see Elisabeth Schüssler Fiorenza, *In Memory of Her* 130–40, 189–91.

79. Cf. ibid. 134; Felix Christ, *Jesus Sophia* 153.

80. *In Memory of Her;* see especially 188–90.

81. Cf. James M. Robinson, "Jesus as Sophos and Sophia," 6.

82. On this see Elisabeth Schüssler Fiorenza, "Wisdom Mythology," 31, 34–35; eadem, *In Memory of Her* 190–91.

83. Cf. ibid. 189–91.

84. See "Wisdom Mythology," 29–31, 33. The author of the Wisdom of Solomon had already composed his book according to the structure of the Isis aretalogies. Philo also received elements of the Isis cult in his writings. See Schüssler Fiorenza, *In Memory of Her* 133, 190–91. Felix Christ also includes a somewhat laconic reference to a connection between Wisdom and Isis (*Jesus Sophia* 154). While the dove originally had no connection with Egyptian Isis, in the Hellenistic-Roman period she may well have acquired this symbolic bird through her increasing identification with Phoenician Astarte, or with Aphrodite (cf. Sarah B. Pomeroy, *Goddesses, Whores, Wives, and Slaves: Women in Classical*

Antiquity [New York: Schocken, 1975] 217–18). For the emancipatory influence of the Isis cult see ibid. 217–26.

85. Only from that point onward was the Holy Spirit regarded as the principle effecting the incarnation (cf. Friedrich Sühling, *Die Taube* 39, and Wolf-Dieter Hauschild's article in *TRE* 12, especially 202ff.).

86. Sühling, *Die Taube* 52–67.

87. Ibid. 53 (cf. this location and p. 195 for Constantine's speech to the synod, in which Pneuma and Logos are also identical).

88. *In Canticum Canticorum hom.* II, 12. Cf. Sühling, *Die Taube* 10–11.

89. Ibid. 15.

90. Ibid. 67–79.

91. Schneemelcher, *New Testament Apocrypha* 1:169. According to the Ebionites Jesus' divine sonship results from the entry of the dove into Jesus, not from a virgin birth. The notion of the union of a heavenly being with the man Jesus to form the Son of God is a clearly Gnostic feature of the christology of this Jewish-Christian group in early Christianity.

92. Schneemelcher, *New Testament Apocrypha* 2:708. For the character, dating, and origins of these writings see ibid. 703–709. See also Sühling, *Die Taube* 70–73.

93. Johannes Geffcken, *Die Oracula Sibyllina* (Leipzig: J. C. Hinrichs, 1902 [reprinted 1967]) 130.

94. Translation in Schneemelcher, *New Testament Apocrypha* 2:722–23.

95. There is also an iconographic tradition corresponding to the idea that the dove remains on the head of Christ. Frequently, in the examples given above, the dove sits on the head of the goddesses (cf., for example, the gold plate from Mycenae in Keel, *Vögel als Boten,* plate 28).

96. Sühling, *Die Taube* 76–77. *Pistis Sophia* is no longer attributed to a Valentinian author, but more cautiously to the Gnostics (of Epiphanius), either Sethians or Severians (on this see Schneemelcher, *New Testament Apocrypha* 1:363).

97. Schneemelcher, *New Testament Apocrypha* 2:470. Cf. Sühling, *Die Taube* 80ff.

98. Ibid. 456–57.

99. Ibid. 446. For the twin young see Ulrich Wilckens, *Weisheit und Torheit* 113 n. 1.

100. Schneemelcher, *New Testament Apocrypha* 1:177. (For the Gospel of the Hebrews see ibid. 172–78.)

101. Quoted from Otto Stählin and Ludwig Früchtel, *Clemens Alexandrinus.* GCS. Vol. 3: *Stromata* VII and VIII etc. (2nd ed. Berlin: Akademie-Verlag, 1970) 108, 112.

102. Sühling, *Die Taube* 77.

103. On this see especially Elisabeth Schüssler Fiorenza, "Wisdom Mythology," 32–33.

104. It is possible that pre-Christian Gnosis also made use of this image as part of its Wisdom speculation. We also may not entirely exclude the possibility that Philo, when he speaks of the dove, has in mind a symbolism with a Gnostic past.

105. Wilckens, *Weisheit und Torheit,* especially 205–13. See also (in connection with the absence of a Passion narrative in Q) Robinson, "Jesus as Sophos and Sophia," 14.

106. Sühling, *Die Taube* 3–4.

107. Cf. Robinson, "Jesus as Sophos and Sophia," 7.

108. Translation by Malcolm L. Peel and Jan Zandee in James M. Robinson, ed., *The Nag Hammadi Library in English* (3rd rev. ed. San Francisco: Harper & Row, 1988) 390. See Max Küchler, *Frühjüdische Weisheitstraditionen* 560.

109. Ibid. 584–86. Cf. Felix Christ, *Jesus Sophia* 154.

110. Cf. Sühling, *Die Taube* 2–6, 52–60.

111. Ibid. 181–91.

112. For the beginnings of Augustinian pneumatology in the idea of love and its immense influence on the doctrinal developments in subsequent centuries see Wolf-Dieter Hauschild's article in *TRE* 12, especially 202–203

113. Sühling, *Die Taube* 183.

114. Cf. Küchler, *Frühjüdische Weisheitstraditionen* 585.

115. Schüssler Fiorenza, *In Memory of Her,* especially 130–40.

116. Ibid. 140–51.

117. Their compatibility is most impressively evident in our pericope, where God-Sophia still speaks in the tradition of the First Testament Servant of God thematic.

118. Schüssler Fiorenza, *In Memory of Her* xx.

Acknowledgments

The originals of these essays appeared in the following publications, and have been used by permission:

"Die göttliche Weisheit und der nachexilische Monotheismus" [Chapter 2] is from *Der eine Gott und die Göttin. Gottesvorstellungen im Horizont feministischer Theologie.* QD 135 (Freiburg: Herder, 1991) 151–82 (©Herder Verlag, Freiburg im Breisgau).

"Weise Frauen und Ratgeberinnen in Israel – Vorbilder der personifizierten Chokmah" [Chapter 3] is from Verena Wodtke, ed., *Auf den Spuren der Weisheit. Sophia – Wegweiserin für ein neues Gottesbild* (Freiburg: Herder, 1991) 9–23 (©Herder Verlag, Freiburg im Breisgau).

"Und als der nächste Krieg begann . . . Die weise Frau von Abel-Bet-Maacha (2 Sam 20,14-22)" [Chapter 4] is from Angelika Meissner, ed., *Und sie tanzen aus der Reihe. Frauen im Alten Testament* (Stuttgart: Katholisches Bibelwerk, 1992) 145–54 (©Verlag Katholisches Bibelwerk).

"Abigail – eine kluge Frau für den Frieden" [Chapter 5] is from Karin Walter, ed., *Zwischen Ohnmacht und Befreiung. Biblische Frauengestalten* (Freiburg: Herder, 1988) 92–99.

"Die personifizierte Sophia im Buch der Weisheit" [Chapter 6] is from W. Dietrich and M. A. Klopfenstein, eds., *Ein Gott allein? 13. Kolloquium der Schweizerischen Akademie der Geistes- und Sozialwissenschaften 1993* (Fribourg: Universitätsverlag, 1994) 543–57 (©Universitätsverlag Fribourg), and in the volume of the series "Orbis biblicus et orientalis" with the same title, vol. 139 (Fribourg: Universitätsverlag; Göttingen: Vandenhoeck & Ruprecht, 1994).

"Jesus Sophia" [Chapter 8] is from Doris Strahm and Regula Strobel, eds., *Vom Verlangen nach Heilwerden. Christologie in feministisch-theologischer Sicht* (Fribourg and Luzern: Exodus, 1992) 113–28 (©Editions Exodus).

"Der Geist, die Weisheit, und die Taube" [Chapter 9] is from *FZPhTh* 33 (1986) 197–225.

General Index

Index of Biblical References